Foreword by Dr. George O. Wood

GOODBYE CHICKEN HELLO DOVE

*Releasing Your Fears by
Welcoming the Holy Spirit's Power*

TIM ENLOE

Goodbye Chicken, Hello Dove:
Releasing Your Fears by Welcoming the Holy Spirit
By Timothy N. Enloe

Enloe Ministries
Holy Spirit Conferences
P.O. Box 780900
Wichita, Kansas 67278-0900
USA

www.enloeministries.org

ISBN: 978-0-9997469-0-5
Library of Congress Control Number: 201791912

Also available in ebook format.
Third Printing.

Contents

Contents

Goodbye Chicken • Hello Dove

Acknowledgements

To Rochelle—

Twenty-five years of marriage and traveling as a family in itinerant ministry have gone by so fast. There have been many days of overwhelming victory and fulfillment; there have been many days of overwhelming warfare and discouragement. Through all of these highs and lows, you—my best friend, spouse and dedicated ministry partner—have stood beside me sharing every intense moment with consistent grace and wisdom. Rochelle, I can't thank God enough for you. You are more than the answer to the idealistic prayers I prayed as a teenager for a perfect companion. I love you.

To Braedon, Dolan and Barret—

This book is dedicated to you. As your parents, you are the greatest work of our lives. All three of you have grown up to be amazing men of God with diverse talents and giftings. We are so proud of you and love you deeply. May you continue to grow in wisdom, favor and stature before God and man.

To Our Parents and Family—

Thank you for your constant love and support. You have influenced us in every good way and your contagious example has made serving Jesus our heart's desire.

To Our Ministry Partners—

You have stood with us for so many years, believing in the call of God upon our lives and enabling us to fulfill it. Thank you for your friendship, prayers and support. We love you and cherish your friendship.

To Don Milam—

Thank you for your experienced eye, spiritual insight and friendship. Your guidance and input have been invaluable and our conversations have been most enjoyable. Thank you for sharing your wealth of wisdom with me. Fly Eagles fly.

To Richard Schoonover—

Your editorial gifting has made this book so much better. You are the rarest of combinations, blending academic and technical excellence with a trained theological mind. Thank you.

To Amy Thomas—

Thank you for Sherlocking the manuscript! Thank you for lending your strong gifting and eagle eyes to this project. Rochelle and I deeply appreciate you.

Foreword

Do you have desire to experience God? Then, this book by Tim Enloe is for you!

I think back to my college freshman class in philosophy. My professor, from the country of Greece, had a working knowledge of Plato, Aristotle, and Socrates in addition to the leading philosophers of the Western World. One day in class he outlined the main two ways we learn: cognitive and affective.

Let me illustrate. When my daughter was three years of age, I led her to Jesus while kneeling with her as she was preparing to say her goodnight bedtime prayer. I asked if she wanted to invite Jesus into her heart. She said "yes," and she did, confessing her sins (if you don't believe a three-year-old has sins to confess, then you've not had a three-year-old), and inviting Jesus into her heart.

A few days later I was driving her to pre-school. She was in laying in the back seat, writhing in pain. I asked her what was wrong and she replied that Jesus was kicking her in the tummy. It took me a moment to connect the dots—now that Jesus was in her heart, He must be the one doing the kicking that was causing her stomachache.

That set me to thinking that her cognitive knowledge of God was severely deficient. And, then it dawned on me that her cognitive knowledge of me was also deficient. She didn't know what a doctoral degree was (when she went across the stage to receive her certificate for attending daily vacation Bible school she proudly announced that she too had her doctorate), how tall I was, or what my personal history consisted of. If she were to introduce me, all she could say was, "This is my Daddy."

But, incredibly, she knew me a lot better than people who had only informational or cognitive knowledge about me. Why? Because she had affective or relational knowledge. We call that latter kind of knowledge experiential. And, as a three-year-old, she already had a personal relationship with the Lord, even though cognitively she couldn't have recited the Apostles' Creed or any formal doctrinal statement.

How does this all relate to the book Tim Enloe has written?

He very lucidly lays out who the Holy Spirit is and what He does. This is cognitive knowledge—it's the information you want to have about the One whom we call the Third Person of the Trinity.

Alongside that, however, he integrates the very vital aspect of how you experience the Holy Spirit—the affective side of our relationship to God.

Just as it's possible to know about Jesus but not know Him, so, it is possible for you to know about the Holy Spirit, but not know Him.

Tim Enloe has decades of experience in helping people do both—to know about, and to experience the Holy Spirit. This book will help you experience the Holy Spirit in fresh new ways!

Dr. George O. Wood
Chairman, World Assemblies of God Fellowship

Introduction

When I was fourteen years old, I had an encounter with God while praying. It was not as dramatic as others have perhaps experienced; I was not caught up to heaven in a chariot of fire, nor did I experience some other extra-terrestrial contact, but it was nonetheless significant and life-shaping to me. During this prayer time, I surrendered my future ambitions to the Lord, and I invited Him to use my life for ministry. That is when I distinctly sensed Him speak to me, in a profound-yet-quiet way, that my life calling would be to "teach others about the Holy Spirit."

For over 25 years it has been my joy-filled privilege to attempt to obey that call and teach others about the Holy Spirit in churches, conferences, Bible colleges and seminaries in many nations. I do not say that to brag, but rather to give context to my next statement. Through the years, the most common questions I have encountered have pertained to understanding, receiving and/or operating in the Holy Spirit's power. Answering those questions is the lofty goal of this book, and I hope to do so—however incompletely—in three segments.

The first third of the book is designed to reset our basic understanding of who the Holy Spirit is—and is not—from the Scriptures. This segment of the book tends to be a little more data-heavy, but serves as an important foundation and answers many common questions.

The second third focuses on how other people received the Spirit's power in the Bible and, in turn, how we can receive this power today. Biblical precedents enable us to follow the clearly-marked path that God has left for us, leading us to the destination He intends. Accurate expectations are so important.

The final third of this book attempts to cover one of the most commonly-overlooked issues in Pentecostal/Charismatic circles, namely, how to put this Holy Spirit power to work in our lives after we have received it. Perhaps millions have received this power over the millennia, and many have done so without knowing what to do afterward. In some ways, this may be the most important—and vulnerable—section of this book.

I hope you sense that the tone of this book moves from information to interaction to inspiration, picking up speed along the way.

Though the subject matter is serious and important, I have chosen to maintain the informal language and speaking style employed while I am teaching a live audience. This has enabled many to relax, absorb and accept the truth of God's Word, then naturally receive His promises in a low-pressure, easygoing way.

My prayer for you is that you not only learn about the Holy Spirit's power, but that you also press in to receive it. Then afterwards, you will continue pressing in to learn how to operate consistently in His supernatural ability.

Tim Enloe

Part One:

All About the Holy Spirit

Chapter One
A Conflict of Birds

Norm was a veteran of the Vietnam War. Tragically, he was exposed to chemical weapons while serving in that horrible war, and the effect of the physical damage to his body was extensive, though I was only aware of the more visible consequences. He was suffering constant, uncontrollable tremors, his walking was very poor and he used a cane to support and steady his gait. While walking, one of his hands gripped his cane while the other held his wife's arm because, though hidden beneath dark glasses, both of his eyes were blind. His wife told me that his eye tissue was so damaged that the whites of his eyes had turned brown and red— and he wore the dark glasses to hide this from others.

He and his wife had recently given their lives to Christ, and I happened to be the guest speaker at the church they were attending. I was speaking over a period of a few days on the topic of the Holy Spirit's power, and both Norm and his wife were beautifully growing in their walk with God.

After the second session, they approached me at the podium. He handed me his cane and said, "Here, I don't want this anymore. Hang it on the podium." With that, he asked his wife to lead him to one of the auditorium's side walls and place his hand on it for a reference point. Then he let go of her steadying, guiding hand and began to tentatively walk a few steps along the wall by himself. His wife and I stood nearby, ready to run to his assistance, but to our surprise, every few steps were less wobbly and were becoming stronger! Before we fully realized what was happening, he was at the back door of the auditorium and was not only walking with a steady pace, but picking up speed! By the time he again circled around to us at the front, he was in a full-speed jog and laughing like a child at a playground.

We were crying and thanking God for the miracle that was happening right before our eyes. After another lap, Norm stopped in front of us, extended his hands out towards us and said, "Look! I'm not shaking anymore!" The decades of tremors were gone too! At his request, we left the cane hanging on the podium for all to see.

The next day, I was in the middle of teaching when a subtle yet urgent inner impression from the Holy Spirit came to me. Though wordless, I could translate it easily as, "Stop teaching. Go down and pray for Norm right now to receive the healing of sight." (I'm sure you have experienced pressure at your job because you've felt overwhelmed and inadequate on some level; I was certainly feeling it at that moment!) The battle began to rage inside me. What should I do? I was in the middle of teaching an auditorium full of people. I did not feel the courage to take the first step; I did not want to risk failing in front of everyone. Trying to collect my thoughts while continuing to speak, this conflict of spiritual urgency and natural fear intensified inside me.

I hate to admit this, but after a few minutes of struggle, I finally had an alternate idea: try to obey the prompting while, at the same time, reducing as much risk as possible. This way, I could technically obey the prompting while simultaneously lowering the chances of looking like a fool if the instantaneous miracle did not happen. It was a peculiar mixture of courage and fear—courage because I could feel the Holy Spirit's presence and fear because I knew I was incapable of performing the miracle this man needed. I felt like such a chicken.

With a tentative voice, I announced to the crowd, "I feel the Holy Spirit's presence here right now; everyone, please, stand to your feet, close your eyes and begin to raise your voice loudly to God right now." The crowd sensed God's presence as well and graciously followed my instructions. When I noticed that no one was looking around, and under the noise of a room full of people loudly praying, I meekly sneaked over to Norm's seat in the second row. Standing in front of him, I said, "Norm, I feel like I'm supposed to pray for you—that your eyes would be healed."

He immediately responded, "I've been feeling that for a few minutes. What took you so long?" I felt my heart sink with failure at his response.

Inward transformation and outward service are the hallmarks of biblical Christianity.

I reached out, placing my hands on his shoulders, and prayed a simple prayer for healing, all the while feeling inadequate and helpless inside. When the prayer concluded, I opened my eyes and looked at Norm, not sure of what to expect, yet hoping for something positive. His dark sunglasses were vacantly staring back at me and there was no change to his facial expression. Realizing that my fear had likely gotten in the way of a life-changing miracle, I began trying to encourage him with a backup "Plan B," namely that we would continue praying and believing with him for a future miracle. However, he interrupted me with this sentence: "That is really strange. I imagined you had blonde hair for some reason; your hair is dark brown—and curly. I can see you."

Then he reached out and firmly pinched the end of my nose! His glasses were off a few seconds later, and his wife was staring intently—in near-disbelief—into his beautiful, restored eyes. The whites of his eyes were now perfect. Norm could not only walk; he could see again, and I was 100% sure that it wasn't because of me.

Ministering in the power of the Holy Spirit does not come easy. It is a lifelong learning process that requires overcoming pride, fear, doubt and indifference, while simultaneously growing in your relationship with Him. While trying to help others, you must constantly be working on yourself, conquering the issues that block you from experiencing the power and freedom of the Spirit.

Behind the Curtain

Do you remember the story of *The Wizard of Oz*? You will not find it in your Bible, but perhaps you've read the book or seen the classic film. The four main protagonists are all searching for something that will fill a void in their lives. The Tin Man needs a heart, the Scarecrow needs a brain, the Lion needs courage. And Dorothy? She just wants to go home. Eventually, after being attacked by flying monkeys, their journey to find what they need leads them to stand before the mysterious and powerful Wizard of Oz. Their initial encounter with the Wizard is a sensory overload, as he presents himself with otherworldly pomp and ominous special effects. Later, however, Dorothy's little Yorkshire Terrier, Toto, uncovers a rather unremarkable man hiding behind a curtain. He is secretly operating the special effects to portray himself as the "The Great and Powerful Oz" when, in fact, he is simply a not-so-great castaway from Omaha. Trying to mitigate the damage from Toto's discovery, he, to no avail, declares through

20

his special amplification system, "Pay no attention to the man behind the curtain!"

Too late, Omaha; your ordinary, unremarkable self is revealed for all to see.

In some ways, I can really identify with this pathetic poser. As Christians, God has innately installed an inner desire for personal transformation and the outward desire to help other people experience a similar transformation. The problem is that we do not possess the power to succeed in achieving those aspirations. We cannot do it on our own. Wisdom eludes us in our attempt to navigate the inner complexities that overwhelm us. We need help to help others, and we desperately need help for ourselves. The resulting angst between what we want to do and what we cannot do creates a great tension within. Confronted by this personal sense of helplessness, we are tempted to camouflage our insecurities and pride behind a masquerade of the super ego, very much like the mighty Oz.

The Wizard of Pride makes us think we are bigger and better than we really are, resulting in this kind of egotistical narrative, "I'm not broken; I'm more whole than you. I can help you. Pay no attention to the ordinary person behind the curtain." This veneer of self-confident pride negatively affects the accurate perception of our own need as well as our sense of how we can help others. Consider these two issues.

First, we look at people dealing with the same kind of issues that plague our lives and condescendingly say, "I feel so bad for those poor people." Like the bloated Pharisee who praised God that he was better than others (Luke 18:9-14), we hide behind self-deceptive curtains. Second, many Christians look at the need around them and hide behind the curtain of indifference that results in apathy. Paralyzed by their overwhelming inner sense of inadequacy and helplessness, they have become disconnected from a world longing for someone to touch them. Both are manifestations of the self-created mask that either elevates ourselves above others or causes us to descend below what God says about us—either way our sense of self rules over what God has clearly said about us in His Word.

Once again, you and I are our own nemeses. Should this surprise us? Probably not. Since the Garden of Eden, we have had an inclination to eat selfish apples and then hide when accountability comes our way. We desire to eat the fruit that exalts us higher than we really are, rather than being willing to expose our own nakedness and humble ourselves before God. Once exposed, we prefer hiding, rather than unmasking ourselves.

Since the Garden of Eden, we have had an inclination to eat selfish apples and then hide when accountability comes our way.

We all need help, right? In fact, we not only need help, we need *supernatural* help! Inward transformation and outward service are the hallmarks of biblical Christianity and yet are also two areas that our human pride consistently fights against. Whether we are masking our personal deficiencies by telling others, "Pay no attention to the man behind the curtain," or playing a game with God as we seek to excuse ourselves from reaching others, our greatest fear is that we will be exposed.

Fear is the cloud hovering over the Christian life, whether it be fear of transforming ourselves or reaching out to help others. How many Christians can recognize that, though the Dove of the

Holy Spirit has descended on them, there is still a powerful chicken lurking deep within?

Do you want to be a Christian who stops hiding behind the curtain of pride and indifference? Do you want to stop playing the religious game of minimizing your personal need for transformation by maximizing the problems of others? Do you want to live a life dependent on the Holy Spirit, rather than on your own natural strength? Do you recognize that you barely know the Holy Spirit, yet desperately need His help to do these things? Are you tired of fear ruining your walk with God? Are you ready to say, "Goodbye chicken; hello Dove"?

If you answered yes to the above questions, fasten your seat belts; this book is for you.

"When we pray for the Spirit's help ... we will simply fall down at the Lord's feet in our weakness. There we will find the victory and power that comes from His love."

Andrew Murray

"O Holy Spirit, descend plentifully into my heart. Enlighten the dark corners of this neglected dwelling and scatter there Thy cheerful beams."

St. Augustine

Goodbye Chicken • Hello Dove

Reflection questions:

1. What are the two ways pride seems to manifest itself in our lives?

2. What are examples of each in your personal experience?

3. What are the hallmarks of biblical Christianity?

4. How does fear try to limit these hallmarks?

Chapter Two
Introducing the Dove

Abandonment is one of the strongest negative experiences humanly possible; it can generate incalculable fear. Hannah Moore, an English writer and philanthropist, asked, "Who can tell the end of fear?"

I will never forget the conflicted feelings Rochelle and I experienced when our middle son, Dolan, had to have ventilation tubes surgically put into his ears. He was only two years old, and his repeated ear infections demanded another course of action beyond repeated antibiotic treatment. Even though it was a routine, minor surgery, it was major to us because he was our son. When the outpatient surgery day arrived, we brought our toddler son to the hospital. He was still rather sleepy. Even though we tried to prepare him for what was coming, he had no real idea of what was actually about to happen.

We entered the waiting room, signed the final paperwork and were escorted to an exam room. My heart still slightly races when I think of the moment the nurse came and asked us to hand over our son. When I extended my arms to pass his cuddling body to the nurse, he erupted in tears and panic! I do not think that he had adequate understanding that this arrangement was temporary, and the look of betrayal and abandonment in his eyes was vivid. Rochelle and I teared up as they took him from the room. Hearing his cry becoming more distant was yet no less heart-rending. In about forty minutes, we were called back to the recovery room where he awakened from anesthesia a few minutes later. Immediately, he sat up crying and terrified, but when he saw us, his panicked expression subsided and his arms shot out towards us. I'm not sure that we had ever been cuddled so closely before by him; and, to be totally honest, we had likely not held him so closely before either. The crying quickly subsided into deep sighs of relief as he tightly held onto us, sensing that his security and identity had been restored. The separation was over. And the procedure was successful.

Fear

Fear is a feeling, an automatic response induced by perceived danger or threat. Throughout Scripture, we encounter men and women who found themselves in situations that frightened them and tempted them to feel abandoned. In a similar way to the story of our son, Jesus knew what was best for His disciples, and it demanded separation. Separation, not abandonment, was imminent, but He would not leave them alone.

The disciples' lives and vocations had been turned wonderfully upside down in the three and one half previous years. Laying aside fishing nets and other professional aspirations had been richly rewarded by being eyewitnesses to miracles and personal mentoring by the Messiah Himself. However, Jesus was increasingly hinting that a change was coming, and coming soon. What would this new era look like? It certainly could not be better; how could anyone top resurrections or transfiguration? Not only would they miss the otherworldly signs and wonders, but also the wisdom, teaching and intimacy of walking with God incarnate.

Fully grasping the idea that He was leaving was a process. And, like the story of our son, He would be passing them into the arms of another for their good. The fear of abandonment and of the unknown must have consumed them. What would their next steps be?

Jesus perceived the state they were in—a state of terror. At the Last Supper, with the disciples gathered around Him, He addressed the paralyzing dread that gripped them. In John chapters 14-16, Jesus spoke to their fear, but more importantly, He opened the door to a new spiritual reality that would address the panic of being left alone. With clarity and intensity, He introduced them to the Holy Spirit.

In chapter 14, Jesus first dealt with their fear of abandonment. Yes, He was leaving. However, He would not leave them alone. At that point, Jesus encouraged them with this announcement. He was going to send them the Holy Spirit, another Comforter, who would eventually be both

Fear is a feeling, an automatic response induced by perceived danger or threat.

"with" them and "in" them. In chapter 15, He set the stage for the task that was before them, to bear witness of Him and bear much fruit, thereby fulfilling the will of God. He encouraged them to understand that the Holy Spirit would help them to accomplish this. Finally, in chapter 16, He wrapped up His message on the Holy Spirit by unveiling several specific ways the Holy Spirit would be with them and help them, emphasizing that the Spirit is trustworthy.

In John 14:15-26, Jesus made His first compelling statement about the Spirit.

If you love me, obey my commandments. And I will ask the Father, and He will give you another Advocate, who will never leave you. He is the Holy Spirit, who leads into all truth. The world cannot receive Him, because it isn't looking for Him and doesn't recognize Him. But you know Him, because He lives with you now and later will be in you (John 14:15-17).

I am telling you these things now while I am still with you. But when the Father sends the Advocate as my representative—that is, the Holy Spirit—he will teach you everything and will remind you of everything I have told you (John 14:25-26).

The NLT uses the word "Advocate" to translate the original Greek noun *parakletos*. *Parakletos* comes from the two words *para* and *kaleo*, together meaning "someone called alongside to help." Other English versions translate *parakletos* as Comforter, Helper and Friend. Outside of Scripture, this word commonly had legal connotations, as in an advisor or friend who would give a character witness or wise counsel, however, it does not mean "attorney."[1] Also notice that Jesus said the Holy Spirit would be "another Advocate," inferring that Jesus was currently their

---

[1] Gilbrant, Thoralf, and Ralph W Harris. *The Complete Biblical Library, Volume 15 Greek-English Dictionary, Pi-Rho*. Springfield, MO: Complete Biblical Library, 1990. Print (63).

Advocate and that the Spirit would continue this work. The apostle John also used this word in his first epistle when he says,

> But if anyone does sin, we have an advocate (*parakletos*) who pleads our case before the Father. He is Jesus Christ, the one who is truly righteous (1 John 2:1).

Notice how John again identified Jesus as Advocate. He is showing that the Spirit will continue the assistance that Jesus had previously offered to the disciples. Jesus was not abandoning them or, like our son experienced, passing them on to some unknown surgical nurse. He was passing them onto another one like Himself who would continue to care for and nurture them, teaching, convicting, reminding and assisting them in their journey. The Spirit was not a stranger; they did not need to fear abandonment.

Jesus then increased His sense of urgency:

> But now I am going away to the one who sent me, and not one of you is asking where I am going. Instead, you grieve because of what I've told you. But in fact, it is best for you that I go away, because if I don't, the Advocate won't come. If I do go away, then I will send Him to you. And when He comes, He will convict the world of its sin, and of God's righteousness, and of the coming judgment. The world's sin is that it refuses to believe in me. Righteousness is available because I go to the Father, and you will see me no more. Judgment will come because the ruler of this

world has already been judged (John 16:5-15).

Here, Jesus was assuring them that when He went away, He would indeed send the Advocate-Spirit to them; they would not be left alone. He further explained that the Holy Spirit would not only affect Christ-followers, but would also affect the lost. The Spirit would bring them to the point of convincing in regard to three separate yet related areas: personal sin, God's perfect sinlessness and the judgment that is coming.

> There is so much more I want to tell you, but you can't bear it now. When the Spirit of truth comes, He will guide you into all truth. He will not speak on His own but will tell you what He has heard. He will tell you about the future. He will bring me glory by telling you whatever He receives from me. All that belongs to the Father is mine; this is why I said, 'The Spirit will tell you whatever He receives from me' (John 16:12-15).

You can almost hear the intensity coming to resolution in these words of Jesus. They only knew the bare minimum at this point and needed much further instruction, but the Holy Spirit—"the Alongside One"—would pick up where Jesus left off. What a relief! He then assured the disciples that the Spirit would not lead them in a different direction or speak from a different perspective. He would continue the ministry of Jesus by relating everything that Jesus wanted to say to them. The Spirit was (and still is) 100% trustworthy.

That last verse (16:15) has meant so much to me over the years; it is loaded with information about who God is and how He works in our lives—perhaps more than any other single sentence in the Bible. We will explore this more in a minute, but first, let's look at *who* the Holy Spirit is.

Who is the Holy Spirit?

There is much confusion about who the Holy Spirit is and what He wants to accomplish in our lives. It is entirely normal for us to struggle identifying with the Holy Spirit. As Dr. George O. Wood once told me, "His first name is 'Holy,' which means 'perfect'—and, if I'm honest, I do not identify with perfect. His last name is 'Spirit,' which means 'invisible'—so I cannot see Him."

The use of words Spirit or Ghost (Ghost is an archaic and perhaps poor translation of the Greek word "Spirit") only make the Dove seem more elusive. It is difficult to get a personal sense of who He is and how He works in our lives.

Trinity

When we talk about the Holy Spirit with others, we often assume that they have a grasp on who the Spirit is and what the Scripture reveals about His being. But many find it rather confusing to understand the Trinity and the place of the Holy Spirit within the Godhead.

It is difficult to speak of the Holy Spirit without contemplating the word "trinity." Although this word is never used in the Bible, the principle it represents is revealed throughout Scripture. Trinity is a word invented by theologians to help explain the nature of God. We understand that He is one being having three distinct Persons within that one being. The root word of trinity is "unity," and the prefix is "tri" (meaning three).

The Bible reveals two main facts about God's nature as it relates to the Trinity. First, as Christians, we worship one God: the eternal God of the Bible. We are mono-theists. He is first revealed to us in the Old Testament book of Genesis as Creator; He is further revealed throughout the rest of the Scriptures as holy, loving, and a host of other divine characteristics.

The most important fact about the Trinity is that our God is one being, one entity, one substance.

There are two main facts concerning the Trinity—or how the being of God is comprised. The most important fact about the Trinity is that our God is one being, one entity, one substance.

The Hebrew *Shema* is an ancient confession of monotheism (belief in only one god) and is recorded in Deuteronomy 6:4:

Hear, O Israel! The Lord is our God, the Lord is one!

In the above verse, the first word *shema* is the ancient Hebrew word meaning "to hear" or "listen to this announcement." The Hebrew word translated into English as "Lord" in this verse is *YHWH* or *Yahweh* (often mispronounced as *Jehovah*). It is the Hebrew name for our God. To this day, out of fear of committing blasphemy, devout Jews will not write or say the name YHWH, Yahweh or God.

Another way of translating this verse is, "All of Israel, listen to this important announcement: We only worship the God Yahweh; He is one being." It is a declaration of monotheism that stands in sharp contrast to other prominent religions of the day, including the many gods worshipped by the nearby Egyptians, Canaanites and Philistines.

This early confession of faith champions the truth that God is one being. This is the most important fact about the composition of God as it relates to the Trinity. As Christians, we worship one God—the God of the Bible, not many gods.

This second fact is subordinate to the first but nonetheless important. God is so vastly superior to us that He does not fit into one puny idea of human conception. According to Scripture, He has revealed Himself to us in the three eternally distinct persons of the Trinity: God the Father, God the Son (Jesus) and God the Holy Spirit.

The second most important fact about the Trinity is that there are three distinct persons within the one being of God.

This information about the three persons of the Trinity (or Godhead) helps us to know much more about who our one God, Yahweh, is.

The reason I bring up this lofty concept of the Trinity is because a misunderstanding of this dramatically affects how we view the Holy Spirit.

When it comes to the Trinity, we can relate to the idea of God the Father. Whether you knew him or not, whether he was a hero or a dud, everyone has a dad. Many envision a white-haired, scowling-faced, angry geezer on heaven's throne when they think of "Our Father in heaven," but we must be careful to not project our negative experiences or conclusions onto Father God; that mental picture is not accurate. Even though we may have some misunderstandings, everyone can—in some way—identify with the person of God the Father.

Then certainly, we can identify with the second person of the Trinity, Jesus the Son of God, because identifying with humanity was one of His most important roles. The Gospel of John says that Jesus "became flesh and dwelled among us." (John 1:14). We can identify with the person of Jesus because He chose to identify with us.

We also identify with Jesus because we have seen paintings of Him, likely of a wimpy, gaunt, pale-faced Northern European Jesus with hippie hair—wearing a robe with an electric blue sash and retro sandals. I'm being a bit silly, but there is some reality to how art has inaccurately affected our image of Jesus. If you want the most accurate description of Jesus, go to Revelation where John the apostle describes what the glorified Christ looks like:

> And standing in the middle of the lamp-stands was someone like the Son of Man. He was wearing a long robe with a gold sash across His chest. His head and His hair were white like wool, as white as snow. And His eyes were like flames of fire.
>
> His feet were like polished bronze refined in a furnace, and His voice thundered like mighty ocean waves. He held seven stars in His right hand, and a sharp two-edged sword came from His mouth. And His face was like

the sun in all its brilliance (Revelation 1:13-16).

The bottom line is that we can more easily envision or relate to the persons of God the Father and God the Son on some level because of the more concrete (however often metaphorical) descriptions mentioned in the Bible.

When it comes to identifying with the third person of the Trinity, God the Holy Spirit, many of us either draw a blank or draw an entirely wrong picture based on misconceptions.

If you mix the dove, oil and fire metaphors, you nearly have the makings for a decent fried chicken dinner—not an accurate understanding of the Spirit of God.

If I asked you the first thing that comes to mind when you think of the Holy Spirit, what would you say? A dove? Oil? Fire? It's true that on one occasion, at the baptism of Jesus, the Holy Spirit took on bodily form like a dove, but the Bible does not show this ever happening again. It is true that He is represented as oil, fire, wind and water in the Bible, but He is not greasy and will not burn you—neither will He blow you down or drown you. Each of these representations and symbols only portray a small characteristic about the Holy Spirit; you cannot apply every quality of every symbol to the Spirit. For example, if you mix the dove, oil and fire metaphors, you nearly have the makings for a decent fried chicken dinner—not an accurate understanding of the Spirit of God.

There are no pictures of the Holy Spirit. In fact, His name removes that possibility. As mentioned earlier, His first name is "Holy" meaning "perfect," and none of us—with all of our human frailty—can easily identify with that concept. His last name is "Spirit," functionally meaning invisible. This removes the possibility of us having a visual image of Him.

Misconceptions about the Holy Spirit

Since we do not have any visual concept of the Holy Spirit, we often try to define Him by His activity—or the activity for which other people blame Him. When some think of the Holy Spirit, they muse about some prank-loving sprite that loves to upset the status quo—and ruffle our dignified appearance. There we are—sitting in church, minding our own business—when suddenly that heavenly practical joker zaps us with His mischievous Taser gun. Now, in an out of control state, we interrupt the service by standing up, waving our hands wildly while shouting unintelligible words and spritzing those seated nearby with tears. We finally return to our senses a few days later, finding ourselves staggering in the drainage ditch by the church—in tattered clothes and with a large bean can stuck on our head.

Those who tend to view the Spirit and His ministry in this way are viewing Him through the eyes of fear, confusion or misunderstanding. They often live their lives trying to stay under His holy radar, much like a child trying to avoid eye contact with a school bully. This perception of the Spirit is not biblical and will dramatically limit a Christian's potential.

Others simply think of the Holy Spirit in Deist terms. He has power—and got the world spinning—but is now basically disinterested in His earthly project. He currently resides in a heavenly retirement home and devotes His time to enjoying creamed corn and shuffleboard. Those who view the Holy Spirit this way see Him as disinterested, distant and disconnected from human experience. Why would you want to waste time trying to interact with someone with whom you could never relate or who could not care less about you?

And yet others view the Holy Spirit's ministry as a one-time event; He only works at the moment of our salvation, delivering a lifetime-sized crate of supplies—without the potential for any further interaction or customer support. Like a vaccination that never needs a booster shot, there is no further anticipation of experiencing the Spirit's supernatural ways or character trans-formation in their lives. This mindset views the Holy Spirit as a delivery service, not a person within the being of God. When we understand that the Holy Spirit is God Himself—not merely a supernatural commodity—it allows us the anticipation of person-ally interacting with Him.

The Biblically Accurate Picture of the Spirit

We can accurately identify and understand the nature and activity of third person of the Trinity, the Holy Spirit, because the Bible gives us much information on who He is and what He constantly wants to do in and through us.

The Holy Spirit is God's personal Spirit.

The Holy Spirit is God's personal Spirit. He is not a regional manager, temp worker, executive assistant or lookalike; He is God. He is as much God as the persons of the Father or Son. You can trust Him just as much as you trust Jesus—after all, He is the "Spirit of Jesus" (Acts 16:7).

Here are some of the ways the Bible describes the Holy Spirit:

Spirit of God	Genesis 1:2
Spirit of the LORD	Judges 3:10
Good Spirit	Nehemiah 9:20
Holy Spirit	Psalm 51:17
My Spirit	Joel 2:28
The LORD's Spirit	Micah 2:7
Spirit of Truth	John 15:26
Spirit of Jesus	Acts 16:7
Life-Giving Spirit	Romans 8:2
God's Spirit	Romans 8:15
One and Only Spirit	1 Corinthians 12:11
His Holy Spirit	2 Corinthians. 5:5
Spirit of His Son	Galatians 4:6
His Spirit	Ephesians 3:5
The Spirit Who Makes You Holy	2 Thessalonians 2:13
Seven-Fold Spirit	Revelation 1:4

As you can see, we are talking about the supernatural Spirit of the one and only God—God's personal Spirit. The Bible assures and reassures us that the Holy Spirit is God Himself and that He has good things for us—good things that we desperately need!

I like the way the great theologian, Gordon Fee, describes the Holy Spirit. "If the church is going to be effective in our postmodern world, we need to stop paying mere lip service to the Spirit and to recapture Paul's perspective: the Spirit is the experienced, empowering return of God's own personal presence in and among us, who enables us to live as radically eschatological people in the present world while we wait for the consummation."[2]

The Holy Spirit is Already There

Much more than theory or theology, God has sent the Holy Spirit to stand alongside us and help us in any way we may need it—even in complex or unique situations.

Several years ago, I was ministering in the African nation of Tanzania. We had also been filming a short documentary highlighting the desperate need for clean water, capturing incredible footage. We were overjoyed at the favor that had been extended to us in remote regions and how powerfully the video footage conveyed the humanitarian crisis there. Certainly, this footage would raise both funds and awareness. This joy, however, was short lived. The day before we had to fly home, we were robbed and the video was stolen. No one was injured, but days of filming and spectacular footage were lost. There was no way to recapture the lost video because of how distant and remote the filming location had been.

I was sitting in the hotel lobby, drinking some coffee, sulking, distraught and frustrated at the negative turn of events. I rehearsed the robbery over and over again in my mind, wondering what could have been done differently to spare the footage.

After a few minutes, a man sat down beside me, offering a cordial greeting. I had seen him several times in the hotel before, and I respectfully replied asking how he was doing. Once again, he warmly responded and asked me how I had been enjoying his beautiful country. At that moment, my guard fell down, and I

---

[2] Fee, Gordon. *Paul, The Spirit and the People of God*. Peabody, MA: Hendrickson Publishers, 1996. Print (XV).

related to him how much we loved Tanzania and were trying to help with the water crisis there. I continued to explain how favored we had been to capture footage explaining the crisis to outsiders who would likely assist with donations, but with the footage now stolen, that aspect of our trip had apparently been in vain. He apologized profusely and thanked me for trying to assist people in the region with the water crisis. Then his phone rang, he excused himself and quickly walked away.

The Holy Spirit is standing alongside you and I right now, ready to continue the ministry of Jesus.

As I was continuing to marinate in coffee and disappointment, this gentleman returned. He asked me if I had a few hours free before our departure flight. I was not sure how to answer because I did not know why he wanted to know my itinerary. Very guardedly, carefully and yet politely, I asked what he had in mind. He explained that he would like to help me recapture the footage and had contacted several people to assist me. Then he handed me his business card. He was the member of the Tanzanian Parliament representing the area we were trying to help! I was sitting next to the person who had the power and authority to help us. The next afternoon, he personally escorted us to areas that desperately needed water and helped us interview village leaders. In a matter of a few hours, we had all of the video that had previously taken days to film. We had *carte blanche* permission to film and, unimaginably, had captured even better footage than had been stolen!

I had been guarded in replying to his question, but he was our answer to prayer. While I was sulking and disappointed, God had sent someone to stand alongside me and help in my time of crisis. In a similar way, many have kept their guard up to the Holy Spirit, because they have not realized that Jesus has sent Him to stand alongside and give supernatural assistance.

Even though it was hard for the disciples to understand, Jesus had to leave, but He would not leave them alone. He would send another Advocate to stand alongside them and help, continuing His ministry to them. The Holy Spirit is standing alongside you and me right now, ready to continue the ministry of Jesus.

How could you welcome more of His help right now? Ask Him. Put the book down for a few moments and welcome Him to reveal Himself and His help to you. He is here.

Now that we are biblically sure that we know the Holy Spirit is both God and good, what does He want to do in our lives?

"God is triune; there are within the Godhead three persons, the Father, the Son and the Holy Spirit; and the work of salvation is one in which all three act together, the Father purposing redemption, the Son securing it and the Spirit applying it."

J. I. Packer

"Those in whom the Spirit comes to live are God's new Temple. They are, individually and corporately, places where heaven and earth meet."

N. T. Wright

Goodbye Chicken • Hello Dove

Reflection questions:

1. What do you think it was like for the disciples to first hear that Jesus was leaving?

2. What could some of their logical and emotional responses have been?

3. Do you feel that you take full advantage of the Holy Spirit's "alongside" ministry?

4. What are some practical ways you could welcome more of His help?

Chapter Three
What the Dove Does

I pray that after you have read this book you will be easily able to tell someone else not only who the Holy Spirit is, but also what He wants to accomplish in our lives as Christians.

John 16:15 has been my favorite verse for many years. It could possibly be the single verse that reveals more about who God is and how He works than any other single verse in Scripture:

> All that belongs to the Father is mine; this is
> why I said, "The Spirit will tell you whatever
> He receives from me."

This reveals how the Holy Spirit's ministry assists us in accessing God's supernatural help and in receiving spiritual insight from the Holy Spirit.

The Ceiling

I would like to visually try to explain this verse to you. The diagram below shows a horizontal line marked "ceiling of the natural realm." Below that line, you will notice the words "human ability." This ceiling refers to the highest potential ability of humanity—the maximum potential of human wisdom, skill and ability. Humans can do incredible things in many different fields

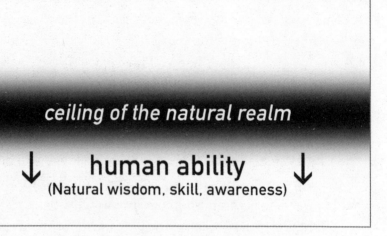

such as aerospace, science, engineering, education, research, etc. Perhaps you are still alive today because of an advanced medical procedure or pharmaceutical discovery. We can build the highest buildings and dig the deepest tunnels; we can explore distant planets in our solar system and send minuscule cameras and robotic instruments into the human body to remotely explore and repair its functions. However, as humans, we have limitations.

While human ability is great and at times seems endless, it indeed has some divinely-imposed limitations. For example, the Bible speaks of God-imposed limitations on creation such as the curse (Genesis 3:14-24), maximum lifespan (Genesis 6:3) and impending judgment (Hebrews 9:27; Romans 14:10). No matter how much our technology advances, human ability can never enable us to ascend to the higher realms occupied by the Creator. Suffice it to say, we can put a man on the moon, but we cannot ever seem to rescue Gilligan from his lost place on the island.

We feel other kinds of human limitations when we experience moments of helplessness. I think we have all struggled with these before on some level. Perhaps the surgeon came into the waiting room to tell your family that he or she could do no more. Maybe your job was unexpectedly downsized. It could be that an unforeseen calamity caused great loss to you or to your family. These—and others like them—are the moments we can tangibly feel the ceiling of the natural realm heavily over us. We are helpless to puncture that ceiling without supernatural help.

If you look below, you will notice an addition to the diagram: God ability. Unlike human ability, which can only operate beneath the ceiling of the natural realm, God's ability is unlimited and can operate freely above and below that line. We cannot get to God without His help; the good news is that He wants to help us. But how?

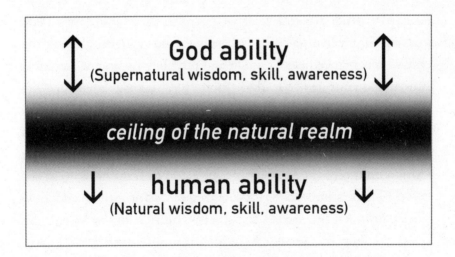

Are you ready to multitask? While thinking about this diagram, try to remember our discussion about the Trinity a little while ago. Then look at my favorite verse, John 16:15 again:

All that belongs to the Father is mine; this is
why I said, "The Spirit will tell you whatever
He receives from me."

From above the ceiling line, Jesus takes all that the Father
has for us and, by His Holy Spirit's ministry, punctures that barrier
ceiling of the natural realm. The Spirit then reveals to us whatever
we need from God.

Do you see it? We receive all that God has for us through
His Holy Spirit. The words of Jesus explain to us that the Spirit is
the One who enables us to receive from God. He is the one who
can puncture the ceiling of the natural realm. This is how desperately we need Him!

Three Main Ministries of the Holy Spirit

Whether we realize it or not, the Holy Spirit has been
working in our lives even before we were born again. He was the
One who convinced us of our sin and revealed the urgent, personal
awareness of our need for God (John 16:8). He was then the One
who washed us and made us new at our conversion (Titus 3:5). As
we discussed, He is intrinsically tied to everything that Jesus does
in our lives, yet many Christians seldom think about welcoming
Him to do more.

There seems to be two extremes relating to if and how
Christians open themselves to the Holy Spirit. On one side, there
are those who live with a bare minimum mentality. They are
practically living under the assumption that every Christian gets
only two or three "Holy Spirit Miracle Wild Cards" to carefully,
calculatedly use during their lifetime. Unfortunately, like wishes
from a genie, they tend to get wasted before they are really needed

(like that time as a child when you contracted poison ivy on your uvula and pled for a miracle, or that Christmas Eve when you prayed and found that front parking space at the mall). This sort of bare-minimum expectancy reaps bare-minimum interaction with the Holy Spirit.

The other extreme is living with a "spiritual ambulance chaser" mentality where you are crisscrossing the country every weekend to find the next new thing. There are some crazy experiences that would boggle the mind. "I've heard they have been supernaturally parting baptismal waters in Missoula and are experiencing levitation in Levittown." Please do not misunderstand me; I know God does bizarre and mysterious things. The Bible contains some incredibly fantastic stories and I've personally experienced otherworldly encounters. However, what I am trying to say is that too many people are living a life of spiritual imbalance where they are constantly chasing what God does rather than God Himself. I understand that an occasional pilgrimage is a biblical concept—and necessary, but we must be careful to keep it in proper perspective. God feels no pressure to constantly outdo His last miracle with something bigger and better. Our spiritual appetites and pursuits should reflect this. That being said, we should also try to maintain a cultivated openness to the out-of-the-box workings of God. Balance is the key.

These two extremes on the spectrum of our openness to the Holy Spirit can dramatically reduce our Christian growth and potential. One side lives generally under-powered, and the other lives generally over-distracted, and both miss the mark. Our goal as a Christian is to receive all that God has for us—whether overtly miraculous or seemingly mundane.

I am not saying that we should expect to see visions of Jesus every day, but I'm also not saying that we should never expect such encounters. Christianity is a supernatural faith, and we are wired with supernatural desires to fulfill our supernatural destinies. The Holy Spirit wants to help us access God's supernatural power so we can fulfill His will for our lives.

Is the ultimate hope of Christianity to barely drag our war-torn carcasses through the pearly gates by the skin of our teeth on some golden daybreak? Or are we designed to live a life of divine interaction and intervention? If we do nothing to change, we will stay in neutral and live a life of spiritual minimums. If we begin to rely more upon the Holy Spirit's ministry, we will live a life of spiritual maximums; the choice is ours.

Is the ultimate hope of Christianity to barely drag our war-torn carcasses through the pearly gates by the skin of our teeth on some golden daybreak?

The Scriptures reveal at least three general categories of the Holy Spirit's ministry that we can experience in our lives; each one is essential for us to consistently experience if we want to live a life of spiritual maximums and access the supernatural. All of these categories are available for each of us to experience.

1. Supernatural Purification

When you hear the word "purification," what comes to mind? A strainer? A water or air filtration system? Purification is simply the process of making something pure. In this case, the Holy Spirit is the Purifier and we are the ones needing a detox. Remember, we are not talking about the human ability to make something pure—below the ceiling of the natural realm; we are referring to a supernatural process. The Bible reveals that humans are entirely incapable of purifying themselves enough to be presentable before a holy God. We cannot atone for our own sins. We need divine assistance from above that ceiling of the natural realm.

Two Levels of Purification

There are two different levels in the supernatural purification ministry of the Holy Spirit. One happens at the moment of salvation, and the second is designed to be a lifelong process afterward.

Have you ever taken care of a swimming pool? If so, you are probably familiar with the importance of chlorine. It is the primary chemical used in many pools to purify the water. There are two concentrations of chlorine utilized for pool care. You use one when you open the pool (after having it covered during the winter), and you use the other for maintaining the pool daily during the summer. When you open the pool at the beginning of the swimming season, it can be surprising how impure the covered water has become. To bring rapid purity to the water, you add the concentration of chlorine often called "shock." You do not use this high-intensity version of chlorine for daily maintenance; it is too strong for routine use. Daily maintenance requires the much lower intensity, standard concentration of chlorine.

In the same way, the Holy Spirit purifies us in two basic levels—when our pool is first opened (when we are saved), we are "shocked" with radical purity and the infusion of a new nature. Later in life, we are progressively purified in a more gradual way to help us stay pure. Theologians call these two levels "Initiation" and

"Sanctification." Initiation is the work of the Spirit at our salvation moment, where He radically purifies us, makes our spirit come alive, imparts a new nature to us, comes to live inside of us and joins us to the body of Christ. Sanctification is the lifelong process after salvation of growing in purity and holiness. God is always calling us to greater levels of devotion that require cleansing and purification for the process. Elizabeth Elliot once said that this process will require a lot of hammering, chiseling and purifying.

Holy Spirit's Purifying Work	Theological Terminology	Effect	Metaphor: Chlorine in swimming pool
Purifying work of the Spirit at the moment of salvation	Initiation *instantaneous event*	Cleansed, made alive in Christ, Holy Spirit comes to live inside	"Shock" in our pool to bring radical, rapid purity
Purifying work of the Spirit following salvation, ideally growing everyday afterwards	Sanctification *lifetime process*	Becoming more like Jesus in our character and nature as we grow in purity	Daily maintenance chlorine in our pool

In Romans 8:9-16, the apostle Paul explains the two basic levels of supernatural purification:

But you [Christians] are not controlled by your sinful nature. You are controlled by the Spirit if you have the Spirit of God living in you. (And remember that those who do not have the Spirit of Christ living in them do not belong to Him at all.) And Christ lives within you, so even though your body will die because of sin, the Spirit gives you life because you have been made right with God.

Therefore, dear brothers and sisters, you have no obligation to do what your sinful nature urges you to do. For if you live by its dictates, you will die. But if through the power of the Spirit you put to death the deeds of your sinful nature, you will live. For all who are led by the Spirit of God are children of God.

So you have not received a spirit that makes you fearful slaves. Instead, you received God's Spirit when He adopted you as His own children. Now we call Him, "Abba, Father." For His Spirit joins with our spirit to affirm that we are God's children.

Paul was emphatic; the Holy Spirit immediately comes to live inside of us at the moment of salvation. When our sinful "pool" is "shocked" by radical, supernatural purification, we are saved and become the temple of the Holy Spirit (1 Corinthians 3:16; 6:19). Again, the Holy Spirit lives inside every Christian from the moment of salvation onward, even if we do not always feel or sense

His presence. He would only leave us if we rejected Christ. As verse 16 above says, "His Spirit joins with our spirit…"

At the moment of our salvation, this work of the Holy Spirit is an amazing miracle. However, this same passage reveals that there is another lifelong miracle of supernatural purification available to us. Paul addressed this letter to people who were already saved, calling the original readers "dear brothers." He reveals that Christians still have a sinful nature (often called the flesh) that wants to regain its rule and reverse the process of purification. I wish when we were saved that all sinful inclination disappeared and we never had another sinful, fleshly desire. If that were the case, then Satan could never again leverage our fleshly weakness as temptation against us. Unfortunately, that is not the case. Right now we are living in the convergence of a strange overlap of two realms; we are saved and belong to God yet we still struggle with the old nature and selfish, fleshly desires. This is the exact reason why we need supernatural help—supernatural purification—*after* we are saved. Perhaps you know what it is like to struggle with some sort of repeated sin issue or sinful bondage in your life. Perhaps a habit or addiction has you living in a cycle of defeat and no matter how hard you try, you cannot seem to overcome its grip. Maybe you feel powerless against overwhelming bitterness or unforgiveness. This is not because your salvation has expired or was inferior to begin with. It is because the old flesh nature wants to again be in control! We can easily discern what is sinful nature/flesh desire because it always involves immediate gratification and leads to long-term destruction.

We are living in the convergence of a strange overlap of two realms.

There are, however, some sin/bondage issues that we can conquer by exercising our own willpower. Some time ago, a man shared with me how he quit a decade of bondage addiction to chain smoking. One day, he picked up his little girl from her first day of preschool and gave her a big welcoming hug. Apparently, her being immersed in an environment without the scent of cigarette smoke had re-acclimated her sense of smell. When she embraced her dad, she pulled away and said, "Daddy, why do you smell so bad when I hug you close?" His heart immediately broke, and in that moment of decision he chose to welcome the warm hugs of his precious daughter, instead of cigarettes. He told me it was tough, but every time he had an urge to smoke, he knew it would cost him the embrace of his young daughter. Human willpower won, and he quit smoking without any drugs, counseling or program. This story demonstrates how sometimes different people can overcome different strongholds by willpower.

We can easily discern what is sinful nature/flesh desire because it always involves immediate gratification and leads to long term destruction.

You have likely overcome some fleshly, selfish inclinations by willpower or positive reinforcement, but we cannot overcome all such inclinations without supernatural help. In fact, many (if not most) sin issues are too powerful for us to face in our own strength.

Paul reminds us that after salvation we are no longer obligated to sin; there is now supernatural power available to us to overcome the most powerful bondage. This is not mere human ability, simply trying harder, nor effort below that ceiling of the natural realm mentioned in the previous diagram. This is divine power that we can access simply because the Holy Spirit now lives in us.

Christians do struggle with sin issues, but thankfully, the apostle Paul tells us how to access this supernatural purification when we are overwhelmed:

> But if through the power of the Spirit you put
> to death the deeds of your sinful nature, you
> will live (Romans 8:13).

Do you see who is responsible for each action? *We* have to put to death the deeds of our sinful nature by utilizing the power of the Holy Spirit. Again, this is not by willpower or our own ability; if we want supernatural results, we must use supernatural tools. God loves to partner with us for His will to be accomplished in our lives. He wants us to act, but act by relying on His power, not ours. In other words, He wants to partner with us to secure our overcoming victory!

So how do we access this supernatural purification that we all desperately need? How do we exert action, but at the same time not act upon our own ability? We do this the same way we accessed the initial supernatural purification when we were saved: we must humble ourselves and cry out to Him in prayer. That may seem overly simplistic on the surface, but our crying out to God reveals our awareness of just how helpless we are without Him. It may not be only one time of prayer that welcomes the Spirit's overcoming power for any given issue. Like taking antibiotics, we may need to cry out several times a day over an extended period of time before the freedom is ours. It is worth contending for any progress we can gain over our sinful nature.

There are, of course, some practical steps we can take to minimize the strength or frequency of overwhelming temptation. When do you sin? What are the circumstances that enable it? Try to avoid those times, places and circumstances—whether they are an actual geographical location or a state of mind.

Did you know that it is possible to be unaware of active sin in your life? Two Scriptures come to mind—and both are very strong. The first is from the apostle Paul when the Corinthian church was challenging him and was comparing him to other spiritual leaders. He wrote:

> As for me, it matters very little how I might be evaluated by you or by any human authority. I don't even trust my own judgment on this point. My conscience is clear, but that doesn't prove I'm right. It is the Lord imself who will examine me and decide (1 Corinthians 4:3-4).

King David wrote a similar sentiment regarding his possible inability to see his own sin:

> Search me, O God, and know my heart;
> test me and know my anxious thoughts.
> Point out anything in me that offends you,
> and lead me along the path of everlasting life
> (Psalm 139:23-24).

The bottom line is that some of the greatest followers of God in the Bible did not always trust their own ability to recognize sin in their lives. How much more careful should we be?

We look at our own spiritual dashboard gauges and everything looks alright; good oil pressure, good voltage. However, just because my personal perception does not see a flashing red light does not mean that there is not a sin process at work that could eventually lead to a major breakdown. I do not say this to cause unjustified fear or paranoia, but sometimes we need an external eye on our inner lives.

When I was a child in elementary school, we had special visitors to our class: a dentist and his hygienist. They showed a short film on how to brush your teeth, then gave us three small gifts afterwards: the world's cheapest toothbrush, a micro-sized tube of generic toothpaste and a small foil packet containing a little red tablet. The tablet contained red dye, and the idea was for us to go home and brush our teeth to the best of our ability. After brushing, our teeth would be sparkling white with no visible issues.

If we want supernatural results, we must use supernatural tools.

Then we were to chew the dye tablet and afterwards, examine our teeth a second time. The red dye would not stick to the smooth enamel of our teeth, but the previously invisible plaque and tartar would absorb the dye and glow bright red. You would go from movie star teeth to zombie apocalypse looking teeth in twenty seconds. It is amazing how the right tool can bring revelation.

Regarding our unseen sins, do you not wish we could have some sort of a tablet we could chew that would expose our undiscovered sin so we could repent and be free? We actually do have something like that available, but it is not in tablet form. Above, King David prayed inviting God to search his heart and test his thoughts. The way we "chew the tablet" is by humbling ourselves and praying, asking God to search us; then we must repent of any sin that He exposes and ask for overcoming help.

Prayer Interaction

Why not put this book aside right now and welcome the Holy Spirit's help in your most difficult or unseen areas? Be transparent and vulnerable to Him. Lower your defenses and prayerfully welcome His help.

"Holy Spirit, I need You! I cannot fight this battle alone; my human resources are inadequate. I cannot do this without Your power and help. Please search my heart and know my thoughts. Reveal any area of sin that I may not see. In some areas, my flesh desires are so strong and Satan entices me with them—I am almost overwhelmed. I welcome Your supernatural power right now; please come and help me. You are stronger than me; please let me be filled with Your strength right now! Please show me any practical steps I can take to reduce or remove or relocate away from this temptation and flesh desire."

2. Supernatural Revelation

There is another major ministry of the Spirit available to help us access supernatural provision from God. This second ministry is all about knowing things that we could not normally know through our broken human understanding alone: supernatural revelation. The Holy Spirit loves to reveal things that will assist us in fulfilling God's will.

Goodbye Chicken • Hello Dove

Earlier we discussed John 14-16, the longest recorded teaching by Jesus on the Holy Spirit. It is important to note that every promise Jesus made about the Spirit's ministry is about revealing supernatural things to us:

"Leads into all truth"	John 14:17
"With you...in you"	John 14:17
"Teach you everything"	John 14:26
"Remind you of everything [Jesus said]"	John 14:26
"He will come to you from the Father"	John 15:26
"Testify all about [Jesus]"	John 15:26
"Convict the world"	John 16:8
"Guide you into all truth"	John 16:13
"Tell you what He has heard"	John 16:13
"Tell you about the future"	John 16:13
"Bring [Jesus] glory"	John 16:14
"The Spirit will tell you whatever he receives from [Jesus]"	John 16:15

Every promise and every verb are about revelation!

Jesus is clear: The Spirit of truth will guide us into all truth. In other words, you can trust the Spirit's leadings. Sometimes His leadings are counterintuitive to our natural mind but are nonetheless trustworthy. And remember, any leading we may sense must always be in line with the Word of God. If we sense a leading that contradicts the Bible, our perceived leading is wrong. The Bible has the final say.

This quote by John Calvin is a bit crude, but it highlights the point that we are not capable of divine revelation without the Spirit. "Man with all his shrewdness is as stupid about under-

58

standing by himself the mysteries of God, as an ass is incapable of understanding musical harmony." Only by the Spirit can we understand the things of God.

Do you remember the hallmarks of biblical Christianity mentioned earlier? They are inward transformation and outward service. To assist in these two goals, the Spirit can guide us inwardly (for ourselves) and outwardly (for helping others).

As Christians, we have access to the Holy Spirit's supernatural GPS from the moment of our salvation. He wants to help us personally follow the will of God. As shown in the Scriptures above, the Spirit provides supernatural revelation resources to help us on a personal level by leading, teaching, guiding, speaking and revealing.

The first supernatural revelation we experience from the Spirit is deeply personal and actually begins before we are saved. John 16:8 talks about the Holy Spirit convincing the world (those not yet saved) of their sin, God's sinlessness and that there is judgment coming. This reveals to us our critical need for a Savior and prepares us to call on Jesus.

However, after we are saved, the Holy Spirit wants to guide us in ever-increasing and constructive ways.

An Unusual Revelation Experience

I began to speak in churches, Bible studies and nursing homes when I was sixteen years old. To say I was inexperienced and green would be an understatement! I was very impressionable and had no formal biblical education aside from attending weekly church services. I did not yet have the wisdom to sort through the contents of a book or sermon and "eat the meat while spitting out the bones." Basically, I would naively accept the contents as being

100% correct. I had no reason to think that a Christian leader or author could possibly be wrong about something. Can you see how desperately I needed supernatural help from the Holy Spirit?

One night after ministering in a small church, I was staying in the guest room of some kind church members. On the nightstand was a book on healing. Because of my passion for divine healing, it really caught my eye. As I went to reach for it, I had an experience unlike anything I had previously known. Right before my hand touched the book, I heard a loud voice firmly say, "No!" The voice was accompanied by a strong inner feeling that something was wrong—sort of like "spiritual indigestion." I do not think anyone else could hear this firm voice, but to me it was most surprising and real. Unsure of what had just happened, I reached for the book a second time and the firm voice again said, "No!" It was also accompanied by the inner feeling of uneasiness. Finally, I reached for a third time with the same "No!" and negative feeling.

The voice was accompanied by a strong inner feeling that something was wrong—sort of like "spiritual indigestion."

I remember saying out loud, "Holy Spirit, you must not want me to read this." I never did touch the book, but because the event was so out of the ordinary for me, I always remembered the title and author. Later I would learn that it was very unbiblical and damaging to many who had read it. The Spirit was protecting me. I am so glad the Holy Spirit helped me avoid being influenced with wrong, damaging understanding at such an impressionable stage in my life. The Holy Spirit wants to guide us on a personal level.

The above experience is more dramatic than the usual ways I have experienced the Spirit's leading. Typically, as I have read the Word and learned more about who God is, I perceive gentle inward nudges of direction and wisdom from Him. Just because something is perceived as more dramatic or spectacular it does not mean it is necessarily more powerful or spiritual. Whether a nudge or an audible voice, hearing anything from the Holy Spirit is important and meaningful!

Prayer Interaction

In what areas of your personal life could you benefit from perfect guidance from the Spirit? Would your marriage, family or relationships be better if you had more supernatural insight from the Holy Spirit? Would you stop reading for just 60 seconds and welcome the Spirit's leading into the most critical areas of your life?

> *Whether a nudge or an audible voice, hearing anything from the Holy Spirit is important and meaningful!*

Holy Spirit, please help me see, hear and feel Your leadings. I desperately need Your help. Teach me to hear Your voice in my everyday life so I can follow You more naturally. Please take all that Jesus has and make it known to me. Guide me in my personal life with greater clarity than ever before.

3. Supernatural Ability

Along with supernatural purification and supernatural revelation, there is a final incredible category of ministry from the

Holy Spirit to us: supernatural ability. While the last category we looked at—supernatural revelation—is partly about helping others, supernatural ability is completely, purposefully aimed at ministry.

After Jesus died and rose again, but before He ascended into heaven, He gave this command to the early Christians:

> But you will receive power when the Holy Spirit comes upon you. And you will be my witnesses, telling people about me every-where—in Jerusalem, throughout Judea, in Samaria, and to the ends of the earth" (Acts 1:8).

He gave this promise to people who had already put their faith in the resurrected Christ. They had been saved in the complete New Testament way in which we have been saved. They, like us, already had the Holy Spirit living inside them from the moment of their salvation, and yet Jesus was promising them a new dimension of the Spirit's work. He was going to empower them with more ability to do more outward ministry. Remember, Jesus had already commanded every believer to do ministry in Matthew 28:19:

> "I have been given all authority in heaven and on earth. Therefore, go and make disciples of all the nations, baptizing them in the name of the Father and the Son and the Holy Spirit. Teach these new disciples to obey all the commands I have given you. And be sure of this: I am with you always, even to the end of the age."

Why would they—and we—need supernatural power to do ministry? Because the task is too big; we are too incapable and too afraid. We are more apt to believe in the chicken's weakness than the Dove's strength. There are five common reasons why we are afraid to personally obey the command to minister to others; all are based on our self-oriented, chicken-like fears:

1. I do not have the time or opportunity;
2. I do not have the resources;
3. I do not have the education/skills;
4. I do not know what to do;
5. I will make mistakes.

The Dove's supernatural ability counters these paralyzing fears with the ability and resources needed to ascend above that limiting ceiling of the natural realm. He punctures through our ceiling of limitation and supplies divine resources for natural people to do supernatural things. He wants to help us accomplish what He has called us to do!

There are other words used for this supernatural ability, commonly called "the anointing of the Holy Spirit" or "the empowering of the Holy Spirit." Within this category of the Spirit's supernatural ability to minister, we call the essential experience prophesied in the Bible the "baptism in the Holy Spirit" (or "Spirit baptism" for short). Spirit baptism is a major prophecy made about Jesus by other prophets as well as Jesus Himself.

For example, we find the prophecy that Jesus will "baptize in the Holy Spirit" is made six times in the Gospels and Acts:

Biblical Usage of Phrase "Baptize In the Holy Spirit"	
Matt 3:11	Prophecy about Jesus by John the Baptist
Mark 1:8	Prophecy about Jesus by John the Baptist
Luke 3:16	Prophecy about Jesus by John the Baptist
John 1:33	Prophecy about Jesus by John the Baptist
Acts 1:5	Prophecy by Jesus about Himself
Acts 11:16	Acknowledgement by Peter

Notably, this prophecy is one of the most repeated about Jesus in all the Bible. Even Peter remembered and quoted this prophecy again in Acts 11:16 after watching a bunch of Italian Gentiles experience this gift.

Consider this: People were first able to be fully born again (or saved), in the completely revealed New Testament sense, only after the resurrection of Jesus. Up to that time, they were still under the Old Covenant (or perhaps in the feathered edges between the Old and New Covenants). After His resurrection from the dead, Jesus suddenly appeared to the apostles while they were hiding in a locked room. When they saw Him and believed in His resurrection, they too were born again in the full New Testament sense. John 20:22 records this moment, "Then He breathed on them and said, 'Receive the Holy Spirit.'" At that moment, the Spirit came to dwell in them (a benefit of New Covenant salvation). After this event, Jesus still promised them that He would baptize them in the Holy Spirit, giving them supernatural power to minister (Acts 1:4-5; 8). Do you see it? There is always more of the Spirit available to us! He wants to help not only in inward transformation but in outward ministry as well. Spirit baptism is an immersion that empowers us for serving the King.

Prayer Interaction

Would you pause for a moment and welcome more of the Spirit's ministry to your life?

Spirit of Jesus, I welcome You now. Would You please help me to see that You are more generous than I have understood? Would You please let me experience Your supernatural ability either for the first time or in an increased measure?

Like the diagram in the beginning of this chapter shows, the Holy Spirit punctures the ceiling of the natural realm and sends supernatural purification, revelation and ability to help us fulfill God's will for our lives. Thank God that He extends supernatural help to natural people!

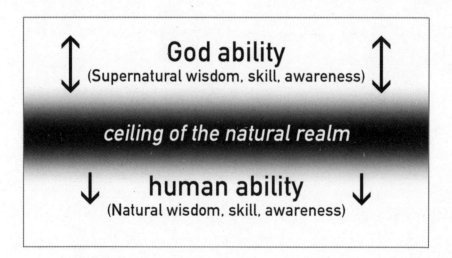

"The Christian religion begins in a New Birth in the power of the Spirit. It is developed under His guidance, and sustained by His presence."

Samuel Chadwick

"To the individual believer indwelt by the Holy Spirit there is granted the direct impression of the Spirit of God on the spirit of man, imparting the knowledge of His will in matters of the smallest and greatest importance. This has to be sought and waited for."

G. Campbell Morgan

Reflection Questions:

1. What are the three major ministries of the Holy Spirit toward us? *Supernatural purification, Supernatural revelation, Supernatural ability*

2. Can you give a personal example of some of the ways you have experienced His supernatural help?

3. What supernatural help are you presently needing?

Part Two:

All About the Holy Spirit's Power

Goodbye Chicken • Hello Dove

Chapter Four

Supernatural Ability in the Old Testament

Several days ago, I was looking through some old family videos. They were many years old and originally recorded on an obsolete standard definition camera. I hooked up the old equipment to our TV and began to play the footage. As a confessed nostalgia junkie, I was filled with warm feelings as I watched the distant memories come to life again. Afterward, I disconnected the ancient standard definition player and tuned to a current channel to make sure I had properly reconnected the cables. The sudden, dramatic improvement in the picture quality was shocking. High definition colors were so much richer; the clarity and depth of the picture were dramatically improved. I had forgotten how limiting the old way had been.

Thinking about this experience, I would like to take you on a short trip back to the standard definition days of the Old Testament. This journey will help you understand the stark contrast between the Old Testament era compared to that of the New. It will also assist you to thoroughly appreciate the dynamically vivid colors of our present Holy Spirit experience now possible in this New Testament age.

Goodbye Chicken • Hello Dove

The first promise of the Spirit's empowering for the purpose of ministry happened early, in the fourth book of the Bible, the Old Testament book of Numbers.

The Old Testament books are under a different spiritual "time zone" than the New Testament. The Old Testament prophetically set up the people of God to be able to identify the coming Savior/ Messiah, while the New Testament reveals specifically that Jesus is the Savior/Messiah whom we have been longing to know. The Old is full of types and symbols, foreshadowing Jesus and His plan that would be later revealed in the New Testament. In the Old, things were very different and often only partially developed. The empowering ability of the Spirit being poured out upon people is one such developing issue.

The Way It Was

Things were very, very different in the Old Testament. There are three very significant general conditions stipulating how the Holy Spirit empowered people back then. Understanding these stipulations sheds a whole new light on the New Testament ministry of the Spirit that we now enjoy.

General Old Testament Conditions for Spirit Empowering:

1. The Holy Spirit's empowering was for special leaders only.
2. The Holy Spirit's empowering followed a basic two-stage pattern.
3. The Holy Spirit's empowering was primarily to benefit the Jewish nation.

70

For Leaders

The category of people we read about being empowered by the Spirit were generally special leaders. The most common roles of these leaders were: prophets, priests, elders, judges and kings. There are roughly 100 people we read about who were empowered with supernatural ability in the Old Testament. There may have been more, but these are the ones recorded in the Bible: Moses, Aaron, the seventy elders of Israel, many judges, King Saul, King David, many prophets and a few others.

This line between specially-anointed leader and the rank-and-file follower was clearly illustrated when Moses ascended Mount Sinai to meet with God in Exodus 19.

> The LORD came down on the top of Mount Sinai and called Moses to the top of the mountain. So Moses climbed the mountain. Then the LORD told Moses, "Go back down and warn the people not to break through the boundaries to see the LORD, or they will die. Even the priests who regularly come near to the LORD must purify themselves so that the LORD does not break out and destroy them" (Exodus 19:20-22).

Moses could meet with God as closely as is humanly possible. While Moses entered God's glorious presence by divine invitation, everyone else was not allowed and they faced severe judgment if they crossed the line. The Old Covenant had a clear line of demarcation between leaders and followers, special and ordinary.

So Close and Yet So Far

I remember as a kid going to a family friend's house for dinner. We were so excited when we saw juicy steaks cooking on the grill. When his parents announced that it was time to eat, we went to the dining room and saw the table set with fine china, and on the table were beautiful steaks and all sorts of amazing side dishes. While preparing to sit down, the parents told us that the kids were eating outside at a picnic table, so I made my way to the backyard. To say I was disappointed would be an understatement! The picnic table had no fine china, no side dishes and no steaks. All that was there were burnt hot dogs on paper plates, garnished by a bag of chips. Talk about a crisp line between two classes!

Can you imagine being one of the perhaps millions of ordinary people at the foot of Mount Sinai?

Can you imagine being one of the perhaps millions of ordinary people at the foot of Mount Sinai (Exodus 19:17-19)? They were distantly seeing God's glory as He descended on the mountain with fire, smoke and an earthquake, yet they could not be near to the God they served. So close and yet so far! They were unable to enter the glory of God while Moses freely could. They were stuck in the backyard eating burnt hot dogs while Moses was in the elite dining room enjoying steaks with God. (If you are a vegetarian, and the meat metaphor is meaningless to you, insert "vine-ripe tomato" in place of "steak" and "rutabaga" instead of "burnt hot dog.")

Later, in Numbers 11, Moses came to a crisis moment because of the "special leaders only" club policy. Do you remember how God supernaturally provided manna for the Israelites to eat in the desert? Do you also remember their response? Complaining. So much so that Moses, the only Spirit-empowered leader, felt so overwhelmed by the ominous task of leading millions of complaining followers that he also began to complain to God:

> I can't carry all these people by myself! The load is far too heavy! If this is how you intend to treat me, just go ahead and kill me. Do me a favor and spare me this misery!
>
> Then the LORD said to Moses, "Gather before me seventy men who are recognized as elders and leaders of Israel. Bring them to the Tabernacle to stand there with you. I will come down and talk to you there. I will take some of the Spirit that is upon you, and I will put the Spirit upon them also. They will bear the burden of the people along with you, so you will not have to carry it alone (Numbers 11:14-17).

Talk about being discouraged; Moses asked God to kill him to take him out of his misery. The people were apparently world-class, gold-medal complainers! Frustration is a normal part of leadership, and if you have led people, you have likely tasted some of this exasperation. Leaders are naturally at least a few steps ahead of those they lead. The answer, as we see in the life of Moses, was not to quit, but to cry out to God for more supernatural help.

Thankfully, God had a better idea than killing Moses. Moses's frustration was a great teachable moment seized by our Heavenly Father. This moment provided God an opportunity to show Moses that when you run out of natural ability you should petition for supernatural help.

To resolve this frustration and its associated difficulties, God gave Moses a specific procedure to be followed. Moses was to select seventy recognized elders (leaders) of Israel and have them stand with him at the Tent of Meeting. Then, in grand fashion, God would speak to Moses in front of them and take the same Holy Spirit who was on Moses and place Him upon the seventy. They would share the workload and would have the supernatural power to get it done. The Scripture notes this taking place with some interesting details:

> And the LORD came down in the cloud and spoke to Moses. Then he gave the seventy elders the same Spirit that was upon Moses. And when the Spirit rested upon them, they prophesied. But this never happened again (Numbers 11:25).

It unfolded almost exactly as instructed, but with one small deviation. Two of the elders, Eldad and Medad, apparently missed their ride to the appointment with the other sixty-eight elders. Even though they were still in the camp with the everyday people, the Holy Spirit fell upon them at the same time as He fell upon the sixty-eight with Moses at the tent of meeting. Even though they were not participating in the special ceremony with the other leaders at a sacred location, God still poured His Spirit out upon them, while they were among the commoners in a mundane location! When word of this breach of protocol arrived to Joshua, Moses's protégé, he was indignant. He asked Moses to restrain Eldad and Medad from doing super-spiritual activity in a super-normal context. He undoubtedly was upset that his inheritance of leadership anointing appeared to be skipping over him and granted instead to a group of third-tier leaders. They were eating steak with Moses, and he was stuck at the kids' table outside!

One day, God would indeed enable all of His servants to be prophetic and allow His Spirit to fall upon them all—not just leaders.

Moses, the man who knew God better than any other human in the Old Covenant, must have surprised Joshua when he responded:

> But Moses replied, "Are you jealous for my sake? I wish that all the LORD's people were prophets and that the LORD would put his Spirit upon them all!" (Numbers 11:29).

This unexpected response from the godliest man on earth foretold and foreshadowed what was to come. One day, God would indeed enable all of His servants to be prophetic and allow His Spirit to fall upon them—not just leaders.

One day, God would indeed enable all of His servants to be prophetic and allow His Spirit to fall upon them—not just leaders.

Goodbye Chicken • Hello Dove
The Two-Stage Pattern of Spirit Empowering

Please note the introduction of a two-stage pattern in receiving the Holy Spirit's power. You will notice these two stages frequently occurring throughout the Bible from this point onward.

Here are the two common stages involved in Spirit empowering:

Stage	Activity	Description
Stage One	"Spirit Upon"	The Holy Spirit falls (rests) upon the person.
Stage Two	"Prophetic (Verbal) Confirmation"	The person speaks Spirit guided words confirming the experience.

Notably, this two-stage process is reinforced three times in this one account: within God's prescription before the event (Numbers 11:16-17), at the actual event (11:25) and in Moses's subsequent comments (11:29). Remarkably, this pattern is repeated over twenty times in the Bible.[3]

In stage two, you may wonder why verbal prophetic speech is elevated to prominence above other supernatural signs. The Bible gives no direct answer, but indirectly we see an important

---

[3] Numbers 11:16-17, 11:25, 11:29; 1 Samuel 10:6,10; 19:20; 2 Samuel 23:1-2; 1 Chronicles 12:18; 2 Chronicles 15:1–7; 20:14–17; 24:20; Isaiah 59:21; 61:1; Jeremiah 1:1-6:9; Ezekiel 2:1–7; Daniel 10:1-19; Joel 2:28-29; Matthew 12:18; Luke 1:67–79; 4:14,15; Acts 1:8; 2:4; 10:44,45; 19:6

indicator. An overview of Scripture reveals that the most common practical outcome of Spirit empowering is verbal. A person needs to speak what God desires them to communicate to others. He wants to most urgently get the word out through His anointed servants to others. Do you see how this applies to the second hallmark of the Christian life: outward service?

For A Jewish Audience

Another significant reason behind prophetic speech as the confirming sign of Spirit empowerment has to do with audience demographics. Prophetic speech is simply saying what God wants you to say in your learned, known language. In the Old Covenant, what people group was the focus of God's attention? The Jewish people. God empowered the Jewish leaders to speak God-influenced words to the Jewish people in the language(s) they understood (Hebrew, Aramaic, etc). It logically follows that an encounter with God, culminating in an experience of God guiding your words, will fill you with courage for future outward ministry.

There were a few exceptional Old Testament moments where God directed His attention towards non-Jews—such as Jethro, Rahab, Naaman, Ruth, Nebuchadnezzar, Darius and the Ninevites. However, these moments are obvious rare variances to the general rule in the Old Testament, revealing the open door that would be offered to the Gentiles in the future. For example, Isaiah prophesies that in a future day,

> You will do more than restore the people of Israel to me. I will make you a light to the Gentiles, and you will bring my salvation to the ends of the earth (Isaiah 49:6).

Even in the Old Testament, God's eventual plan is beginning to unfold, corner by corner, but not yet fully revealed in the Old Covenant. Better days are ahead for the Gentiles, but until then, the central object of God's attention is the Jews.

A Deeper Look at the Two-Stage Pattern

This two-stage pattern becomes even more vivid when you look at how God specifically called and empowered prophets in the Old Testament. Many of the Major Prophets had a nearly identical story of how God empowered them for outward service.

The common narrative begins with an ordinary, unworthy or even obscure person. These unlikely characters have divine encounters with God where they experience Him in a supernatural and supersensory way, then their experience is confirmed with prophetic speech. Based on the confidence gained through that experience, they launch out into great or greater impact.

For example, consider Moses prior to his prophetic calling. He was featured on "Egypt's Most Wanted Criminals" list. He was a murderous felon at large. His mug shot was seen throughout the land. Couple his criminal past with his personal stuttering issue, and you can see why he ran to out-of-the-way Midian to hide from his past. In the desert, two things happened to Moses. God gave him a supernatural encounter (stage one) and then empowered him for new prophetic ministry culminating in a prophetic sign (stage two). Moses had a supernatural encounter with God in front of a burning bush (fully burning, yet not consumed by the fire). In that burning bush, he saw God standing in the flames. Next, he heard God speak. This was followed by the tactile experience of his bare feet on holy ground. This supernatural experience would be followed up by other supernatural signs (for instance, the curing of leprosy on his hand and his staff turning to a snake).

Stuttering Moses then entered stage two of his empowering process when he was empowered to speak with authority. Remember, however, Moses was not very confident to get into the public speaking arena, so God graciously partnered him with his trusted older brother Aaron—for a short time—as training wheels on a bike, allowing Aaron to speak on behalf of Moses. This only lasted for the first few encounters with Pharaoh, at which time Moses took over his rightful place as spokesman on God's behalf. From that point on, he was operating not as an unqualified, less-than-average Moe; he was now a Spirit-empowered prophet.

Prophet	Stage One: Spirit Upon (Supernatural Experience)			Stage Two: Verbal Confirm-ation
	Supernatural Seeing	Supernatural Hearing	Supernatural Feeling	
Moses (Exodus 3:1-4:12)	Burning Bush, Saw God (3:2)	God Spoke (3:4)	Signs (4:1-9)	Empow-ered to Speak (4:12)

We see this same motif is seen in the calling of Isaiah the prophet. In the year King Uzziah died, Isaiah saw the Lord, heard God's voice and felt the supernatural hot coal on his tongue before he was confirmed with prophetic speech:

Prophet	Stage One: Spirit Upon (Supernatural Experience)			Stage Two: Verbal Confirm- ation
	Supernatural Seeing	Supernatural Hearing	Supernatural Feeling	
Isaiah (Isa 6:1-9)	Saw the Lord (6:1)	God Spoke (6:8)	Hot Coal on Tongue (6:7)	Prophe- sied (6:9)

Or consider the priest Jeremiah's divine encounter that transformed him into a prophet: seeing visions, hearing God's voice, feeling God touch his mouth before being confirmed with prophetic speech:

Prophet	Stage One: Spirit Upon (Supernatural Experience)			Stage Two: Verbal Confirm- ation
	Supernatural Seeing	Supernatural Hearing	Supernatural Feeling	
Jeremiah (Jeremiah 1:11- 6:9)	Saw Vision (1:11-12)	God Spoke (1:5)	God Touched His Mouth (1:9)	God's Words in His Mouth (6:9)

The prophetic commissioning experience of the exiled priest Ezekiel while in Babylon follows the same course with visions of the "wheel within a wheel," hearing God's voice, the physical sensations of falling down under God's power and the Spirit entering him prior to the confirmation of speaking God's words:

Prophet	Stage One: Spirit Upon (Supernatural Experience)			Stage Two: Verbal Confirm-ation
	Supernatural Seeing	Supernatural Hearing	Supernatural Feeling	
Ezekiel (Ezekiel 1:1-3:4)	Saw Visions (1:1-28)	God Spoke (1:3)	Fell Down, Spirit Entered (1:28-2:2)	Spoke God's Words (3:4)

The prophet Daniel's experience is nearly identical, with the supernatural experiences of seeing, hearing and feeling other-worldly senses before prophetic confirmation:

Prophet	Stage One: Spirit Upon (Supernatural Experience)			Stage Two: Verbal Confirm-ation
	Supernatural Seeing	Supernatural Hearing	Supernatural Feeling	
Daniel (Daniel 10:5-19)	Saw Heavenly Being (10:5)	Heard Being Speak (10:9)	Fell, Touched, Trembled (10:8,16)	Strength-ened to Speak (10:19)

As you can see, this is a consistent pattern with all five of the major Old Testament prophets.

Let's move on from Numbers and glance at another high point in the Old Testament development that leads us away from the "leaders only" model. The prophet Joel wrote an oracle from God declaring that, in the future, after the Messiah is revealed, the Spirit would fall upon a larger demographic:

I will pour out My Spirit upon all people.
Your sons and daughters will prophesy.
Your old men will dream dreams,
 and your young men will see visions.
In those days I will pour out My Spirit
 even on servants—men and women alike
(Joel 2:28-29).

This protocol-shifting, precedent-setting prophecy unfolds the future of Spirit empowering. Once the Messiah would be revealed, every servant of God could experience what had been previously reserved only for special leaders. No more burnt hot dogs on paper plates; everyone could one day have steak on fine china!

In the future, sons and daughters, young and old, servants and socialites—everyone could potentially experience the two stages involved with Holy Spirit empowering: the Spirit falling upon them and prophetic confirmation. It is interesting to note that hundreds of years later Peter referenced these verses in his Pentecost sermon; he twice quoted Joel's prophecy above, "and they will prophesy," adding it a second time to emphasize his point (Acts 2:18). This reinforces the purpose of the Spirit's empowering, that He desires to speak through us to others.

Notably, even the prophetic experiences of dreams and visions that were once reserved for leaders and prophets would one day become available to anyone—young or old. Any ordinary follower of God would be eligible to receive this long-awaited promise. Age would not matter; gender would not matter; social status would not matter. In the future, none of God's people would have to eat burnt hotdogs!

"Everybody gets to play."

John Wimber

"The Spirit-filled life is not a special, deluxe edition of Christianity. It is part and parcel of the total plan of God for all His people."

A. W. Tozer

Reflection questions:

1. Can you identify with the feeling of being spiritually "left out"? How?

2. Even though you know that the Spirit will now empower any Christian, do you still have an inner feeling of unworthiness? If so, do you think it is biblically justified or just a human feeling?

3. With the limitations of "Jews only" and "Leaders only" removed from the qualifications, what empowered possibilities are available for you?

Goodbye Chicken • Hello Dove

Chapter Five
Supernatural Ability in the New Testament

A change of seasons often brings a new, fresh perspective. This is exactly what was happening as we close the Old Testament books and enter the beginning of the New Testament. As the old winter snows disappeared and the new spring of Matthew, Mark, Luke and John began to blossom, everyone could sense that a bright summer was nearing.

A New Season

Although the old way of the Spirit's empowering had distinct limitations ("leaders only" and "Jews only"), the winds of change were blowing. With prophetic foreshadowing from Moses to Joel, anticipation from the devout people of God had been increasing. Before Jesus was revealed as Messiah, this statement from John the Baptist set the stage:

> Everyone was expecting the Messiah to come soon, and they were eager to know whether John might be the Messiah. John answered their questions by saying, "I baptize you with

water; but someone is coming soon who is
greater than I am—so much greater that I'm
not even worthy to be His slave and untie the
straps of His sandals. He will baptize you
with the Holy Spirit and with fire (Luke
3:15-16).

John the Baptist was resolute; he was not the Messiah. The
Messiah would be much greater than he. John's role was to set the
table for the Messiah by preparing the hearts of ordinary God
followers by encouraging repentance from sin.

Jesus was revealed as the longed-for Messiah, and He
fulfilled His earthly ministry. After His passion, He stirred urgent
anticipation in His followers (who were mostly ordinary people by
Old Testament standards) for the fast-approaching appointment
with the Holy Spirit's power. Just before His ascension back to
heaven, Jesus reminded His followers what was next to come:

"And now I will send the Holy Spirit, just as
my Father promised. But stay here in the city
until the Holy Spirit comes and fills you with
power from heaven" (Luke 24:49.

"Do not leave Jerusalem until the Father
sends you the gift He promised, as I told you
before. John baptized with water, but in just
a few days you will be baptized with the Holy
Spirit" (Acts 1:4-5).

"But you will receive power when the Holy
Spirit comes upon you. And you will be my

witnesses, telling people about me everywhere—in Jerusalem, throughout Judea, in
Samaria, and to the ends of the earth" (Acts
1:8).

The timeframe from the beginning of the Gospels to the
Resurrection in some ways functioned as feathered or tapered
edges between the Old and New Covenants. Christ's death
and resurrection certainly brought an immediate start to the New,
but His previous earthly ministry was the accelerated transition
time—the hopeful spring season between the winter-law and
summer-grace.

Jesus ascended to heaven to fulfill a major promise
mentioned in all four Gospels, namely, that He would baptize His
followers in the Holy Spirit's ministry power. For whatever reason
known only to Him, He had to return to heaven before pouring
out His Holy Spirit's power on His followers. And that is where
the Jewish festival of Pentecost suddenly becomes important.
Pentecost Festival was one of the three most important Jewish
holidays along with Passover and Tabernacles. Every able-bodied
Jewish man was expected to return to Jerusalem to observe the
required rituals and reflection associated with the Pentecost
celebration. These Jewish seasons had great historical and spiritual
meaning. During Pentecost, also known as Shavout, the Jewish
people celebrated two main events: the spring harvest and God
giving Moses the Law on Mount Sinai. This international
pilgrimage feast would be the stage for God shattering the first of
the two Old Testament's two limiting conditions for Spirit
empowering: leaders only.

Acts 2 recounts the events of that amazing day:

On the day of Pentecost all the believers were meeting together in one place. Suddenly, there was a sound from heaven like the roaring of a mighty windstorm, and it filled the house where they were sitting. Then, what looked like flames or tongues of fire appeared and settled on each of them. And everyone present was filled with the Holy Spirit and began speaking in other languages, as the Holy Spirit gave them this ability (Acts 2:1-4).

It is imperative to note who Luke was writing about here; the mention of "all the believers" in Acts 1:14-15, reveals the followers of Jesus at the Pentecost celebration. There were 120 present at the celebration, including the apostles, Mary and her other sons, along with the "women." This guest list in Acts 1 is referencing the week prior to the Day of Pentecost. It is possible that there were more believers empowered by the Spirit on that Pentecost day than just 120. However, it is our best count of who was there.

Of the 120, how many would be qualified under the Old Testament condition of leaders only? Probably only the twelve apostles. If we use our best estimate number of 120, only 10% were qualified by the "leaders only" precedent. Yet, it is clear; the signs "filled the whole house" (2:2), the appearance like fire "settled on each of them" (2:3), and they were "all filled...and began speaking" (2:4). All heard the sound like wind; all saw the appearance like fire; all experienced the inrush of the Spirit's power. All of them, not just the special leaders.

Moses's prophetic desire that one day all could have the Holy Spirit rest on them and be prophets (Numbers 29:11) had come to pass! Joel's oracle (Joel 2:28-29) that the Holy Spirit would be poured out on the formerly-unqualified young, old, men, women, slave and free—non-leaders—became the new norm! God was fulfilling His promise of democratizing the power of His Spirit so everyone could get in on it. Steaks for everyone.

Two Stages Revisited

Do you remember the two-stage pattern of "Spirit upon," then "prophetic confirmation?" That was exactly what happened here. Do you recall the more detailed charts of the major Old Testament prophets from the last chapter? Now the same pattern was happening again, but this time not exclusively to handpicked prophets, but to a group of nameless, average followers of Jesus:

Prophet	Stage One: Spirit Upon (Supernatural Experience)			Stage Two: Verbal Confirm-ation
	Supernatural Seeing	Supernatural Hearing	Supernatural Feeling	
Chris-tians at Pente-cost (Acts 2:1-4)	Saw Flames Like Fire (2:3)	Heard Sound Like Wind (2:2)	Fire Rested Upon Them, Filled with the Spirit (2:3-4)	Spoke in Other Tongues, Then Prophe-sied to Crowd (2:4; 14)

God went so far as to repeatedly and specifically fore-shadow this transition in the Scriptures. He also went to the extreme of selecting the apparently-unqualified, recent denier of Christ, Simon Peter, to be His anointed spokesperson later that day. Peter not only spoke in tongues, but he later spoke to the crowd with prophetic power, with 3,000 embracing Jesus as the Messiah and being baptized. Like special prophets of old, this Pentecost group had together seen supernatural sights, heard supernatural sounds, felt supernatural stimulus and their experience was confirmed with supernatural words. Not bad for a bunch of nobodies.

What was once reserved for a special few leaders is now available for all to experience.

Do not mistake the metaphors for something else here; the text is explicit. There was no literal wind blowing and no actual fire burning; it was the sound "like" wind and the appearance "like" fire. These are timeless metaphors drawing on some of the forces of nature, a common way to describe otherworldly experience in the Old Testament. What was once reserved for a special few leaders was now available for all to experience. The long winter of the Old Testament ways was long gone; the refreshing spring of Jesus's earthly ministry had recently passed and now the warm summer of the church age had dawned. The mission of Jesus would not be fulfilled by only Himself or a few handpicked emissaries; from now on everyone in the church could ascend to a place where they would be a Spirit-empowered army and together fulfill the ministry of Jesus.

When a large crowd amassed around this group of prophetic tongues speakers, some were amazed and astonished, but some began to ridicule them as drunks. Peter quickly stood and answered their astonishment and insult with a rather simple answer:

> These people are not drunk, as some of you
> are assuming. Nine o'clock in the morning is
> much too early for that. No, what you see was
> predicted long ago by the prophet Joel:
> 'In the last days,' God says,
> 'I will pour out my Spirit upon all people.
> Your sons and daughters will prophesy.
> Your young men will see visions,
> and your old men will dream dreams.
> In those days I will pour out my Spirit
> even on my servants—men and women
> alike—and they will prophesy
> (Acts 2:15-18).

The well-known, much-anticipated prophecy of Joel—where one day everyone would have prophetic experience and ministry—was now here. There was a new normal now. Goodbye chicken; hello Dove!

Notable to everyone was that both stages of Spirit empowering had again occurred; the Spirit had rested upon them all and they were all speaking as the Spirit was prophetically guiding them (Acts 2:4).

Do you remember the three general conditions for Spirit empowering in the Old Testament?

1. The Holy Spirit's empowering was reserved for special leaders only.
2. The Holy Spirit's empowering followed a basic two-stage pattern.
3. The Holy Spirit's empowering was to primarily benefit the Jewish people.

The first condition had become obsolete. The prophecies of Moses and Joel were fulfilled; not just special leaders only, but now anyone who was a follower of Jesus could participate and be empowered. Since this empowering was no longer sequestered for the leadership class, it opened doors for a dramatically expanded ministry that potentially had significant impact on the surrounding world. More empowered people could minister to more needy people.

The second and third conditions would be married in a wonderful union and bring fulfillment to Isaiah's many prophecies about Gentiles. Peter himself would prophetically declare them to be a new audience to the gospel:

> Peter replied, "Each of you must repent of your sins and turn to God, and be baptized in the name of Jesus Christ for the forgiveness of your sins. Then you will receive the gift of the Holy Spirit. This promise is to you, and to your children, and even to the Gentiles— all who have been called by the Lord our God" (Acts 2:38-39).

It is important to remember that Peter would not personally understand or adopt the acceptance of Gentiles into the church community until seven years later in Acts 10. The prophetic anointing that fell upon Peter at Pentecost elevated his message to a place that transcended his own bias and misunderstanding! When the Holy Spirit is upon us, the potential is limitless.

On Pentecost, God still used the basic two-stage empowering (Spirit upon, prophetic confirmation)—however, with a slight enhancement. This second confirming stage of prophetic language was not restricted to the Hebrew language, but opened to the many languages of the Gentile world! God was indeed empowering ordinary people to be witnesses in Jerusalem, Judea, Samaria and the ends of the earth (Acts 1:8). God had not forgotten the Jews, but He had opened the invitation to everyone else so all could experience the power and blessing of the Holy Spirit.

Many of the bilingual internationals in the crowd recognized that these 120 rural Galileans were now fluently declaring the "wonders of God" in at least thirteen other recognized languages (Acts 2:5-8). Ordinary people speaking Spirit-inspired words in languages they did not personally understand would be a sign that would be repeated over and over in Acts. Before Pentecost, special prophets would have the Spirit rest upon them, and their ministry anointing (to speak to Jews) would be confirmed as they spoke in Hebrew (or Aramaic). After Pentecost, ordinary followers of Jesus would have the Spirit rest upon them, and their ministry anointing (to speak to the world) would be confirmed as they spoke in the languages of the world. Do you see the utilitarian function?

Today, many of those who have not experienced praying in tongues may misunderstand the motivation of those who practice it. Some think that Pentecostals or Charismatics view this ability to be a badge of spiritual superiority or special recognition. A few uninformed, immature insider-participants may feel this way, but they are not the majority. If you have ever felt like speaking in tongues was an issue of pride or spiritual class distinction, I am so sorry; that is not the case at all. I am so sorry that we have allowed this biblical sign to become distorted, misrepresented and sometimes misused. Often the misapplication of our spiritual practices can lead to the exact opposite outcome of the one we intended.

The reason why we Pentecostals/Charismatics value this experience is because we have found the command of Jesus to do ministry is overwhelmingly difficult without the Spirit's supernatural ability. Speaking in tongues is a sign confirming that we can all now access this supernatural ability. As Acts 2 shows us, if we can trust God to guide us to speak in an unknown language, how much more can we be confident that He will guide our known language to speak to others! Speaking in tongues is a prophetic confirmation of a prophetic experience that empowers us to be prophetic witnesses.

Speaking in tongues is a prophetic confirmation of a prophetic experience that empowers us to be prophetic witnesses.

God wants to empower us generally for outward ministry, but most commonly to speak His words to others. Luke, who wrote both Luke and Acts, used a peculiar word to describe the Holy Spirit guiding our speech. In Acts 2:4, "everyone present was filled with the Holy Spirit and began speaking in other languages, as the Holy Spirit gave them this ability." The word translated "gave them the ability" in the NLT text (or more familiarly "utterance" in the classical King James Version) is the Greek word *apophthengomai*. This word simply means to "speak out with inspiration"[4], and the text states that the Holy Spirit was the One inspiring or prompting them to speak out in tongues. This Greek word is only used by Luke and only used three times, all in his writing of Acts. The second time he used this word is ten verses later, in Acts 2:14, when Peter boldly preached to the crowd in the known language. Luke is obviously using an uncommon term to create a conceptual bridge for his readers. The same Holy Spirit who gave the prompting, inspiration, or words to speak in tongues on a personal level was giving the prompting, inspiration and words to communicate the Gospel on a public level. And Peter was only one of the 120 or so who were identically empowered that day. Speaking in tongues functioned as a confirming sign to them personally of greater verbal ministry to come.

We know that the essential hallmarks of the Christian life are inward transformation and outward ministry. There is no problem understanding the fundamental importance of inward transformation. Why? Because we can all embrace the reality of our own personal weakness. However, we often ignore the

---

[4] Gilbrant, Thoralf, and Ralph W Harris. *The Complete Biblical Library, Volume 11 Greek-English Dictionary, Alpha-Gamma*. Springfield, MO: Complete Biblical Library, 1990. Print (411).

importance of spiritual empowering for the purpose of a prophetic witness rather than embracing it, because of that same personal weakness. Just like the Wizard of Pride hiding behind that curtain, our fears hinder our potential.

So why do we feel so insecure about ministering to others? Because many live under the impression that God can only use someone who has it all together. Do you remember the five common excuses why we try to excuse ourselves from the second hallmark of the Christian life, outward ministry?

1. I do not know what to do.
2. I do not have the training/education.
3. I do not have the resources.
4. I do not have the time.
5. I will make mistakes.

While many—or all these excuses—may be true, the Holy Spirit's power is like a wildcard that can overcome any or all of our fears and inabilities. He knows what to do. He has all knowledge and will lead us. He has all resources at His disposal. He helps us to prioritize and steward our time. He does not make mistakes, but even if we do—if we remain humble and teachable—He patiently helps, navigating us through life with supernatural wisdom and grace. We can either believe our excuses, or we can believe God's promise. When a Christian is baptized in the Holy Spirit, he or she receives supernatural ability to minister. It is time for the chicken to go.

Just to be clear: The reason why God fills people with His Spirit today is so that Pentecostals/Charismatics can speak in tongues and feel superior to their non-tongues speaking Christian friends. No! Not at all!

If you are still not convinced that God would really empower someone like you and me who are not "qualified" apostles or leaders, reflect again on Peter's first statement to the unbelieving crowd at Pentecost. When they accused the raucous bunch of breakfast time drunkenness, without hesitation, Peter explained:

> These people are not drunk, as some of you are assuming. Nine o'clock in the morning is much too early for that. No, what you see was predicted long ago by the prophet Joel..."
> (Acts 2:15).

God was publicly announcing through His spokesperson that now the longed-for shift had occurred. The Spirit's power has now been democratized, available to all, regardless of race, status or intelligence. And Peter then demonstrated this newly-confirmed prophetic power as he boldly spoke and thousands responded by believing in Jesus as Messiah.

After this event, the book of Acts traces the expansion of the Kingdom of God through the Holy Spirit's power. This is traced both geographically ("Jerusalem...Judea...Samaria...to the ends of the earth" Acts 1:8) and racially (Jewish audience, then adding Gentiles).

Certainly, God was still using leaders, notably Peter and Paul. But He was also using deacons, like Philip and Stephen; the common folk, like Barnabas, John Mark and Silas; and others, like the tent making husband and wife team of Priscilla and Aquila. Even the four unmarried (likely adolescent) daughters of Philip are recognized prophetesses in the church. Young and old, sons and daughters, prisoner and free, leader or follower; it is clear we are in a new season. The book of Acts demonstrates this reality, over and over again: winter is over, and the Dove has landed.

Take a moment and look over the completed chart on the following page, reflecting on the unique opportunity to be supernaturally empowered that is now for all Christians to experience.

Prophet	Stage One: Spirit Upon (Supernatural Experience)			Stage Two: Verbal Confirmation
	Supernatural Seeing	Supernatural Hearing	Supernatural Feeling	
Moses (Exo 3:1-4:12)	Burning Bush, Saw God (3:2)	God Spoke (3:4)	Signs (4:1-9)	Empowered to Speak (4:12)
Isaiah (Isa 6:1-9)	Saw the Lord (6:1)	God Spoke (6:8)	Hot Coal on Tongue (6:7)	Prophesied (6:9)
Jeremiah (Jer 1:11-6:9)	Saw Vision (1:11-12)	God Spoke (1:5)	God Touched His Mouth (1:9)	God's Words in His Mouth (6:9)
Ezekiel (Eze 1:1-3:4)	Saw Visions (1:1-28)	God Spoke (1:3)	Fell Down, Spirit Entered (1:28-2:2)	Spoke God's Words (3:4)
Christians at Pentecost (Acts 2:1-4)	Saw Flames Like Fire (2:3)	Heard Sound Like Wind (2:2)	Fire Rested Upon Them, Filled with the Spirit (2:3-4)	Spoke in Other Tongues, Then Prophesied to Crowd (2:4; 14)

"Before Pentecost the struggle was hopeless. After Pentecost, they overcame. The Spirit made slaves into sovereigns, victims into victors, and cowards into conquerors."

Jeffrey Brice

"Since the days of Pentecost, has the whole church ever put aside every other work and waited upon Him for ten days, that the Spirit's power might be manifested? We give too much attention to method and machinery and resources, and too little to the source of power."

Hudson Taylor

Reflection questions:

1. What alignment can you see between how God empowered Old Testament Prophets and the Christians on the Day of Pentecost in Acts 2?

2. Which Old Testament qualifications were wiped away in Acts 2?

3. Can you try to identify with the believers on that day? What might they have been feeling and thinking as they experienced the signs of seeing, hearing, feeling and speaking?

Chapter Six
Jesus, the Dove and Us

I had a rather embarrassing moment that happened in Memphis, Tennessee a few years ago. We were speaking at the historic Memphis First Assembly of God church for a Holy Spirit Conference, and I was unaware of a very peculiar annual event that had just ended there. You probably know that Elvis Presley made his home in Memphis. His mansion, Graceland, is among the most visited tourist attractions there. You may not know that Elvis had a Pentecostal background and had been a member at Memphis First Assembly.

At a certain time every year, Memphis is flooded by Elvis aficionados and impersonators. I have been told that during that time, you can be eating in certain restaurants and be one of the only diners not dressed as Elvis. Some dress up as young Elvis wearing a sports coat and slacks, while others choose to don a white, bell-bottomed jumpsuit complete with a colorful sequin phoenix embroidered on the front. All of them try in some way to grease their hair (or wig) into a dark pompadour like their idol, often adding huge 1970s-era sideburns and dark glasses. During this season, many impersonators visit Elvis's church to complete their experience, and, you guessed it, they come in costume! Can you imagine preaching to your congregation that suddenly has a scattering of 100 or more visiting Elvis impersonators staring back at you?

Sometime after the annual Elvis season, about an hour before our first Holy Spirit session at the church, I walked into the building. By random chance, I was wearing dark slacks and a black sport coat. I had been running late and did not have time to fully dry my hair, so it looked wet, shiny and very black. It was a very windy morning, and from the parking lot to the church door, my hair had been blown wildly until it settled into a meteorologically coiffed pompadour. Once inside, it was my intention to immediately find a men's room and restore my hair to normal. That plan, however, was sidetracked. As I passed through the door, I saw a lady carrying an unusually large stack of boxes and bags. Her arms, torso and head were totally hidden by the cargo. I quickly stepped up and offered to help her carry something. Her face emerged from behind some boxes, and her expression changed from normal to concerned as she politely declined my help and proceeded to walk away. I found a mirror on a nearby wall and fixed my hair before I met with the pastor. We went on to have a wonderful service that morning, with many people experiencing God's power.

After the service, I was talking with church people and had totally forgotten about my brief encounter with the lady carrying the boxes and bags. That is when she found me and apologized for not accepting my offer of assistance earlier. She had not realized that I was the guest speaker and had assumed I was—and I quote, "a very tardy and a very poor-quality Elvis impersonator." Add that to my resume, "Poor-quality Elvis impersonator." She did not say creepy, but that was implied. I have been called a lot of things before, but that one is hopefully a once-in-a-lifetime occurrence. I had not only missed the Elvis migration, but I was additionally not a very convincing double. At that moment, I was so glad I had not worn my white jumpsuit to church.

Add that to my resume, "Poor quality Elvis impersonator."

There are few things more ridiculous than a partial pretender. Why even bother? Go full-on Elvis or stay home. Even worse than a bad impersonator would be a con artist or fraud, someone claiming to be someone else for nefarious reasons. Either way, impersonators are not the person they attempt to emulate.

The Real Thing

When Jesus arrived on the scene, there had been many imposter messiahs, some religious and some military. Like the lady in the Memphis church carrying the boxes, everyone was rather cautious, even leery of pretenders.

Thankfully, the Old Testament gives countless prophecies about the special one who would come and someday fix everything, righting every wrong and restoring people into the presence of God. The composite image of these numerous prophecies helps us identify the real Messiah in the midst of a pool of "poor quality imposters." Isaiah 61 is one such prophecy. It outlines the specific mission that the promised Messiah will fulfill:

> The Spirit of the Sovereign LORD is upon me, for the LORD has anointed me to bring good news to the poor (Isaiah 61:1).

This portion of Scripture shows the single greatest criteria in recognizing the real Messiah: His interaction with the Holy Spirit. Major events in the earthly life of Jesus were marked by interaction with the Holy Spirit:

Christ's Interaction with the Holy Spirit in Scripture	
His Conception	Matthew 1:18, 20; Luke 1:35
His Dedication	Luke 2:25-27
His Forerunner's Announcement	Matthew 3:11; Mark 1:8; Luke 3:16; John 1:33
His Baptism and Anointing	Matthew 3:16-17; Mark 1:10-11; Luke 3:21-22; John 1:32-34
His Guidance to Wilderness Temptation	Matthew 4:1, Mark 1:12, Luke 4:1
His Victorious Return from Wilderness Temptation	Luke 4:14
His Personal Announcement	Luke 4:18
His Miracles	Acts 10:38
His Exorcisms	Matthew 12:28
His Prayer Life	Luke 10:21
His Teaching/Preaching	Luke 4:18; Luke 12:12
His Atoning Death	Hebrews 9:14
His Resurrection	Romans 1:4; 8:11
His Great Commission	Luke 24:49; Acts 1:8

The Scriptures are emphatic! Jesus relied upon the ministry of the Holy Spirit. His role as Messiah was, in many ways, defined by this partnership. In fact, the word "Messiah" comes from the Hebrew word meaning "the Anointed One"—the only one who would fill and could fill this role. What other common name is used for Jesus in the Bible? Christ. Jesus Christ or Christ Jesus. "Christ" is an English translation based on the Greek word *Christos*, which also means "The Anointed One."

> Messiah = "The Anointed One" in Hebrew
> Christ = "The Anointed One" in Greek

This is significant because, by saying "Jesus Christ," you are making a confession of Christian faith, "Jesus is the Anointed One." And this confession is made at least 280 times in the New Testament.[5]

Jesus is the Son of God, the long-prophesied, long-awaited Messiah-Christ Savior. He is the authentic Messiah, not some plastic imposter or cheap impersonator. The whole Bible verifies His authenticity and identity.

In fact, the only time we have record of the Holy Spirit taking on a physical form was at the baptism/anointing of Jesus:

> One day when the crowds were being baptized, Jesus Himself was baptized. As He was praying, the heavens opened, and the Holy Spirit, in bodily form, descended on Him like a dove. And a voice from heaven said, "You are my dearly loved Son, and you bring me great joy" (Luke 3:21-22).

---

[5] Gilbrant, Thoralf, and Ralph W Harris. *The Complete Biblical Library, Volume 16 Greek-English Dictionary, Sigma-Omega*. Springfield, MO: Complete Biblical Library, 1990. Print (527).

In this passage, many scholars discuss the significance of a dove, but please remember that this theophany (or temporary appearance of God to humans) was never repeated. Of perhaps greater significance was the full sensory demonstration of the Trinity associated with the incarnate Jesus, the voice of the Heavenly Father and combined with the momentary appearance of the Holy Spirit like a dove. All of heaven was vouching for Jesus as Messiah.

No wonder Jesus used the Isaiah 61 prophecy to inform His earthly home town of His heavenly identity:

> When He came to the village of Nazareth, His boyhood home, He went as usual to the synagogue on the Sabbath and stood up to read the Scriptures. The scroll of Isaiah the prophet was handed to Him. He unrolled the scroll and found the place where this was written:

> "The Spirit of the LORD is upon me, for He has anointed me to bring Good News to the poor, He has sent me to proclaim that captives will be released, that the blind will see, that the oppressed will be set free, and that the time of the LORD's favor has come" (Luke 4:16-19).

Not only had the forerunner John the Baptist announced Jesus' true identity (John 1:29), but dramatically, the audible voice of the Heavenly Father had done so as well (Matthew 3:17, Mark

1:11). Now, Jesus was erasing any doubt when He read the Isaiah prophecy in public.

> Then He began to speak to them. "The
> Scripture you've just heard has been fulfilled
> this very day!" (Luke 4:21).

Jesus was unmasking His secret identity as the Anointed One, but what did this mean to the people in the audience that day? The idea of anointing someone—particularly with expensive oil—had both concrete and ceremonial meaning to their culture. The concrete meaning had to do with the emollient, moisturizing effects of expensive olive oil on desert-dry skin—a rare luxury. The ceremonial meaning was totally symbolic. There was no magic in the oil. In the Old Testament, special leaders were often ceremonially anointed to celebrate and announce their newly-acquired, special status. The two main ceremonial meanings of anointing with oil were: being chosen and being empowered. When you are chosen (or "set apart"), you are given authority or jurisdiction. When you are empowered, you are given power or ability. Notably, priests and kings were anointed with oil in the Old Covenant; they were each given special authority and power.

When ceremonial oil was poured on your head, it meant much more than just having greasy hair.

When ceremonial oil was poured on your head, it meant much more than just having greasy hair. There was powerful meaning symbolized by the action. You had a new role and the ability to accomplish the role assigned to you.

When Jesus declared that the Holy Spirit was upon Him because the Spirit had anointed Him, it trumped any previous earthly ceremony where a human had anointed someone. Jesus is the paragon of what it means to be anointed. He is uniquely the Christ, the Messiah. Or, as John the Baptist said about Jesus,

> For He is sent by God. He speaks God's words, for God gives Him the Spirit without limit (John 3:34).

Where Do We Fit In?

So how does this affect us? The baptism in the Holy Spirit is the universally available anointing of power available to Christians today. Understanding the anointing of our great example, Jesus, helps us understand our role and frame our expectations.

Do you remember where followers of Jesus were first called Christians? Acts 11:26 tells us it was in Syrian Antioch, where Paul and Barnabas taught the church for a year. It carried the connotation of being a follower or small representative of the Messiah. Astoundingly accurate. We are called to be branch offices of the Anointed One, wherever we may go.

We are called to be branch offices of the Anointed One, wherever we may go.

We are not the Messiah, but rather His followers and representatives. He has the Spirit "without limit" or without measure (John 3:34), but we have only a portion, a deposit or first installment (2 Corinthians 1:22). As Christians, we have likewise been set apart and empowered to continue the mission and ministry of the Messiah. He does not empower us to use His power for our purposes, only for His.

The Purpose of the Anointing

So, what are the purposes of the Spirit's empowering? What did Jesus do and what does He want us to do to continue His ministry today? When Jesus read the Isaiah prophecy above, He was almost reading a job description for His time on earth. There is always a purpose behind being anointed by the Spirit; "The Spirit of the Lord is upon me *because...*" There is a cause behind the anointing: to reveal that Jesus is the Anointed One!

Luke 4:18-19 is only a small portion of the lengthy messianic prophecy from Isaiah 61, but in these few statements we find the essential mission of Jesus and, therefore, the purpose of the anointing of His Spirit:

1. To bring good news to the poor (broken, less fortunate ones);
2. To bring freedom to the captives (bound, oppressed);
3. To bring healing to the blind (sick, afflicted);
4. To bring the Lord's favor (Kingdom of God to earth).

These four purposes of the anointing upon Jesus were systematically and effectively fulfilled in His earthly ministry.

"Good news to the poor," "free the captives," "heal the afflicted" and "bring God's favor" were such welcomed statements, especially in the ears of the Jewish nation that had awaited the appearance of the Messiah. Between the Old Testament and the birth of Jesus were 400 difficult years. Even before that time, during the exile, the Jews had gone through the horror of oppression/occupation by the Babylonians and Medo-Persians. Then, afterward, during the intertestamental period span of 400 years, the Jews suffered under domination by the Greeks and Romans. Even if there were occasional, brief moments of freedom, they were clouded by the fear of constant attack and oppression. The last several centuries, before the coming of Christ, the Jews had endured the pillaging of valuables, poverty, lack and constant fear. There was seldom, if ever, any good news and hardly any hope of freedom.

Even the optimistic attempt at revolt in 165 BC/BCE by the Jewish rebel/zealot Judas Hasmon "Maccabeus" (a nickname meaning "the Hammer")—who was trying to win freedom from the occupying tyrant, Antiochus Epiphanes—was eventually met with a tragic end. Hopes for freedom were crushed. Judas Maccabeus temporarily recaptured Jerusalem with his band of 3,000 revolutionaries and restarted the temple's daily sacrifice for the first time in years.[6] This brief success is still celebrated today in the Jewish holiday of Hanukkah. However, the Maccabean Revolt only lasted about thirty years before any hope of freedom was put down. So close and yet so far; almost good news for the poor, almost freedom for the oppressed people who felt the very opposite of favor. Judas "the Hammer" Maccabeus was not the Messiah as some had thought, and he had not brought good news to the poor or freedom to the oppressed. Like the lady in Memphis's opinion of my accidental Elvis impersonation, Judas Maccabeus was—compared to the real Messiah—just a wannabe with bad timing.

---

[6] Gowan, Donald E. *Bridge Between the Testaments: Reappraisal of Judaism from the Exile to the Birth of Christianity.* Allison Park, Penn.: Pickwick, 1985. Print (80-86).

This was the context in which Jesus announced His identity as Messiah. You can see why this was such a powerful moment. The Jews must have wondered, "Could He really be the Anointed One, or will He be yet another in a line of disappointing impersonators?" Of course, Jesus went on to complete all the Messiah markers—one after another, and often many times over.

The first part of that Isaiah prophecy, "to bring good news to the poor," was about power to speak or proclaim. This is the primary purpose of the Spirit's anointing. Do you remember the two stages of Spirit empowering? The Spirit falls upon us; we then experience verbal confirmation by saying things He is leading us to say. This gift of being empowered by or baptized in the Holy Spirit is primarily and fundamentally about power to speak. The other areas of power include wonderful sub-points. If you ever sense the anointing, you can almost assume that this is what needs to happen. God wants to speak through you so you can minister to others. The prophecy is about proclaiming the Gospel to the broken because they are God's target audience. People who recognize their need are much easier to help. The Holy Spirit anointed Jesus to speak and He wants to anoint us to speak as well.

People who recognize their need are much easier to help.

The second part of Isaiah's prophecy embraces the delivery of freedom to the oppressed or bound. This is not an excuse to plot a prison break, but rather a supernatural avenue for the freedom so many desperately need. We live in a world where people are oppressed and carry heavy burdens. Everyone seems to be a slave to some vice, habit, pursuit or substance. Satan works to keep as many active chains on a person's life as possible: alcoholism, drug addiction, prescription drug addiction, pornography, abuse, materialism, etc. It seems like some people go from one bondage to another, trying to fill a void that they can never quite identify. Going from one abusive relationship to another, one substance to a different kind, one overwhelming fit of rage to yet another will never satisfy the inner void. Only Jesus, the Anointed One, can do this. He is the One who opens prison doors and releases captives; He is the Lord who can conquer the mightiest giants we face.

And what about demonic bondages? We understand that Satan attacks people on a spectrum of intensity that starts with temptation and ends up in complete domination. No matter where someone may be on this spectrum, the anointing is far stronger. Over the years, I have dealt with people in varying degrees of demonization—from oppressed to being fully dominated by evil spirits, sometimes referred to as "possessed." On each occasion, the anointing of the Holy Spirit has proven to be exponentially stronger than any of the enemy's prison locks or hopeless lies. This anointing power of the Holy Spirit is designed to break bondages.

The third purpose of the anointing is power to heal. Whether for physical or emotional issues, everyone needs healing. Scan your memory and considered the many healings in the Old Testament: people were healed of barrenness, leprosy, boils, snake bites and raised from the dead. However, do you recall any healings of the blind, deaf, lame or mute? Those conditions are mentioned, but there are no recorded healings of them under the Old Covenant. And yet Isaiah prophesied these specific healings to be performed by the coming Messiah:

> In that day the deaf will hear words read from
> a book, And the blind will see through the
> gloom and darkness (Isaiah 29:18).

And when He comes, He will open the eyes
of the blind and unplug the ears of the
deaf. Then the lame will leap like a deer, and
the tongue of the mute will shout for joy
(Isaiah 35:5-6).

You will open the eyes of the blind. You will
free the captives from prison, Releasing those
who sit in dark dungeons (Isaiah 42:7).

It is interesting to note that Jesus performed all four of
these miracles—many of them frequently, and often on the
Sabbath—perhaps just to challenge the broken traditions of the
religious leaders. This is quite clear as witnessed in the case of the
man born blind in John 9. The religious leaders would rather deny
the first healing of this condition in known world history than to
acknowledge that Jesus performed it and was therefore the
Messiah. Notice what the healed man said about the historical
precedent of his healing from blindness and what it means about
Jesus:

"Ever since the world began, no one has been
able to open the eyes of someone born blind.
If this man were not from God, he couldn't
have done it" (John 9:32-33).

When John the Baptist was in prison, nearing his execution
by Herod, he sent some of his disciples to find Jesus, wanting a
final confirmation that He was indeed the Messiah. Jesus
responded:

"the blind see, the lame walk, the lepers are cured, the deaf hear, the dead are raised to life, and the Good News is being preached to the poor" (Matthew 11:5).

In other words, these specific miracles were designed to identify the Messiah. And wonderfully, we read of these miracles continuing in the Early Church in Acts long after Jesus ascended to heaven.

We are not called to mimic His wardrobe or hairstyle; we are called to emulate His character and continue His mission. Both are to be done by relying on the Holy Spirit.

Parallel to my strange encounter in Memphis, Jesus is the One everyone really wants to see. Though He is certainly not dead, He is not physically on the earth today. We are not called to mimic His wardrobe or hairstyle; we are called to emulate His character and continue His mission. Both are to be done by relying on the Holy Spirit. It would be tragic if those around us only saw a caricature or pathetic attempt at checking a few cosmetic, religious boxes. The world needs to see that Jesus is the Anointed One through the anointing of the Spirit that enables us to represent Jesus and powerfully demonstrate His identity.

The fourth purpose of the Spirit's anointing is to proclaim or reveal that the favor of the Lord has come. But what does this mean? For millennia, the Jewish nation experienced some dramatic negatives: they were oppressed in slavery, homeless in desert wanderings, had to fight for their land, dealt with warring invaders, were prisoners in foreign captivity, punished for and by immoral leaders, experienced civil war, etc. Please understand that there were positive times too, but the majority of time that extended through several thousand years of history, the nation did not live under what anyone would call "favor." The political kingdom of Israel was not a clear representation of the Kingdom of God on the earth. But when Jesus began His ministry, He brought heaven's Kingdom and possibilities with Him. In John 3, He met with Nicodemus and explained that there is a spiritual, non-material Kingdom that has now come. How does one enter and enjoy that Kingdom? The answer is clear. To enter the kingdom, you must be born again:

> Jesus replied, "I tell you the truth, unless you are born again, you cannot see the Kingdom of God...I assure you, no one can enter the Kingdom of God without being born of water and the Spirit" (John 3:3,5).

The Kingdom of God is the place of His favor. It is invisible with no physical border. It is not a specific location, but can be in any place where people embrace Jesus as the Anointed One.

When Jesus came to earth, He ushered in a new and better covenant. George Eldon Ladd vividly explained that the Kingdom of God was the rule of Christ upon the earth; and that His Kingdom was more of a reign than a realm.[7] In other words, anywhere Jesus is welcomed is a place of favor, and the Kingdom has

---

[7] Ladd, George Eldon. *The Gospel of the Kingdom: Scriptural Studies in the Kingdom of God*. Grand Rapids, MI: Eerdmans, 2001. Print (19-22).

arrived. When Jesus made this announcement in Nazareth, He brought with Him His Kingdom favor. Anything was now possible because the King was now here. No longer would there be the walls and protocols of the Old Testament law separating us from God's intention for us. Though He would retain His full divinity, God Himself would also take on our humanity and bring His Kingdom to us! His reign would transcend geography, thus having no earthly limits.

When you and I are saved, we are brought into His Kingdom. After this spiritual experience, when we go to work or school, we bring His Kingdom favor with us. God is now with us and His Kingdom power and authority are also here. The favor of the Lord has come.

With the advertised availability of such favor demonstrated in power proclamation, healing, deliverance and the arrival of God's Kingdom, you might wonder how to access them. Are they just museum displays, or can we handle them? The Dove descended upon Jesus, but will He also descend upon us? Are we destined to be true representatives or "poor impersonators" who look like their Mentor but possess none of His abilities? Let's look closely at this connection to the anointing.

Connection

How can we get connected to this anointing so we can continue the ministry of Jesus? What equipment is needed? A defibrillator? Jumper cables? An Elvis costume? Thankfully, no. Jesus promised that we "receive power when the Holy Spirit comes upon [us]" (Acts 1:8). In context, that promise is directly tied to receiving Spirit baptism. The first part of the necessary connection is getting baptized in the Holy Spirit. Unless Jesus lied, which He is incapable of doing, then Acts 1:8 is true, and it records the words of Jesus that we will receive power at this defining moment. Remember, Spirit baptism is an anointing of power and authority for ministry. This empowering from the Dove for outward service enables us to overcome the chicken inside, but we need to learn how it works. We are confidently connected to the Spirit's anointing when we are baptized in the Holy Spirit.

An interesting question is raised at this point. Can a Christian who has not been baptized in the Holy Spirit operate in some level of His power and anointing? I have read arguments on both sides, but I have found the Bible is always the best place to find the answer. Let me propose a portion of Scripture that can help us solve this dilemma: the entire Bible before Acts. People were first fully baptized in the Spirit in Acts (chapters 2, 8, 9, 10, 19), yet we read of the Spirit's power flowing through Old

Can a Christian who has not been baptized in the Holy Spirit operate in some level of His power and anointing?

Testament prophets, priests, kings, elders and judges. In the New Testament, we read of Simeon and Anna, Zechariah, John the Baptist, Mary, the twelve disciples, the seventy others, etc. These experiences with the Holy Spirit happened before Jesus had baptized one person in the Holy Spirit. I believe the answer is simple; God can do whatever He wants to do. Yes, a Christian can operate on some level in the Holy Spirit's power before he or she is baptized in the Spirit. However, there is always more to experience and enjoy. Spirit baptism dramatically increases this anointing and power in our lives. The issue is our desiring the maximum, not being satisfied with the minimum. And, for the sake of balance, we must always remember that Spirit baptism is not designed to be a one-time event, but rather a lifelong, growing adventure (see Acts 4:23-31; Ephesians 5:18).

When in doubt, go back to the words of Jesus. He said we receive power at Spirit baptism, so His words trump any of our experiences. Whether you have or have not experienced some level of anointing power before being baptized in the Spirit, receiving now will grant you more. Lots more.

But what about the other side of the connection? We must connect to needy people, that is everyone on earth because everyone has needs. How do we connect to the myriad of needs around us every day? How do we know when we are supposed to talk to or pray with someone? Will God suddenly cover our mouths with His chloroform rag and render us unconscious, seize control of our bodies and make us minister? Then, when the event has passed, wake us up in a church lobby, wondering what has happened? Not likely. Ever. God has always wanted us to participate with Him by our choice in inward relationship and outward service. He really does not make us do anything by force. Technically, He could, because He is God and has all power, but biblically this is not His usual way of interacting with us. We must learn His ways and then courageously step out and follow His leading.

One of the biggest roadblocks to having this anointing power flow through our lives is our perception of the prompting to minister. Many read the account of Philip with the Ethiopian eunuch (Acts 8) and assume that spectacular prompting is the common instigation to reach out to someone else. They build a doctrine of "divine appointments," figuring that there may be a few of these significant moments in life where you experience overwhelming Holy Spirit compulsion. Otherwise you are just "on call," with no responsibility to act unless God sends up a flare. Nothing could be further from the truth! First, there is no indication in the text that Philip had an angelic appearance, burning bush experience or alien abduction. The Scripture records rather casually, with no great fanfare:

> The Holy Spirit said to Philip, "Go over and walk along beside the carriage."

> Philip ran over and heard the man reading from the prophet Isaiah. Philip asked, "Do you understand what you are reading?" (Acts 8:29-30).

Philip heard and obeyed. We do not even read that the Spirit told him the first thing to say. He knew he needed to approach this foreign visitor. In fact, Philip's response may have been more dramatic than the prompting he received. The Spirit told him to walk, but he ran! He was apparently excited about the opportunity before him, confident of the miraculous way God had used him earlier in Samaria. He had learned to discern the Spirit's voice in his life and gained confidence in the purposes and power of the anointing (to speak, free, heal or release God's Kingdom). We, too, must learn these skills through prayer, devotion and childlike attempts to show the love of Jesus. The signal to minister may be faint or overwhelming, but we must obey nonetheless.

Considering the Philip narrative and in light of the other ministry events in the New Testament it is important to consider this question: In the Gospels and the book of Acts, just how many ministry moments were motivated by a recognized Holy Spirit prompting? In the context of all, less than one third have a direct compulsion by God to minister. Most of the time it was simply the Anointed One or an anointed one responding to the needs around them crying out for help. For example, look at only five of the many examples from the ministry of Jesus in Mark's Gospel:

> Suddenly, a man in the synagogue who was possessed by an evil spirit began shouting, "Why are you interfering with us, Jesus of Nazareth? Have you come to destroy us? I know who you are—the Holy One of God!" Jesus cut him short. "Be quiet! Come out of the man," He ordered (Mark 1:23-25).

> Now Simon's mother-in-law was sick in bed with a high fever. They told Jesus about her right away. So He went to her bedside, took her by the hand, and helped her sit up. Then the fever left her, and she prepared a meal for them (Mark 1:30-31).

> A man with leprosy came and knelt in front of Jesus, begging to be healed. "If you are willing, you can heal me and make me clean," he said (Mark 1:40).

> Four men arrived carrying a paralyzed man on a mat. They couldn't bring him to Jesus because of the crowd, so they dug a hole through the roof above His head. Then they lowered the man on his mat, right down in front of Jesus (Mark 2:3-4).

> When Bartimaeus heard that Jesus of
> Nazareth was nearby, he began to shout,
> "Jesus, Son of David, have mercy on
> me!" (Mark 10:47).

In each of these cases, Jesus was simply responding to the needs around Him; there is no obvious leading other than someone crying out for help. Or, consider two more examples from Acts:

> [The lame beggar] asked them for some
> money Peter and John looked at him intently,
> and Peter said, "Look at us!" The lame man
> looked at them eagerly, expecting some
> money. But Peter said, "I don't have any
> silver or gold for you. But I'll give you what I
> have. In the name of Jesus Christ the
> Nazarene, get up and walk!" (Acts 3:4-6).

> Publius's father was ill with fever and
> dysentery. Paul went in and prayed for him,
> and laying his hands on him, he healed
> him. Then all the other sick people on the
> island came and were healed (Acts 28:8-9).

In each case, the apostles were responding to the needs around them, with no obvious compulsion from the Holy Spirit.

Over the many years of our ministry, people have presented this excuse to me countless times: "I was baptized in the Holy Spirit a long time ago but have never felt any leading to witness or minister." These friends totally misunderstand the nature and operation of the Holy Spirit's anointing! Whether you sense a leading or not, whether you feel goosebumps or not, you have been anointed to minister and commanded to do so by the Anointed One. Waiting around doing nothing is not an option. Some are afraid of being presumptuous by acting without some sort of significant or spectacular leading, but that is backward. It is presumptuous for us to not act upon the promise, experience and command that Jesus has so clearly given to us.

The way we complete the connection of the anointing is by staying connected to God while we reach out with love and compassion to those around us and allow the anointing to flow through our lives.

Some are afraid of being presumptuous by acting without some sort of significant or spectacular leading, but that is backward.

Have you ever played telephone with two empty soup cans or two paper cups and a long string? You poke a tiny hole in the bottom of each can or cup and feed one end of the string through the hole, then tie a knot so it will not fall out. You then repeat the process on the other side, so you have a can or cup attached to either end of the string. You have a friend put their ear against the open end of the can or cup, and then you talk into the open end of yours. If the string is pulled tight, it is amazing to hear the low-fidelity transmission of sound vibrations through the string, into the listening side. But if you should happen to let the string become slack, the sound vibrations are absorbed by the loose string, and no transmission can be heard. Flowing in the anointing is similar. One soup can represents God, the other represents the person in need, and the anointed person is the string. Our job is to reach out to God in personal devotion and confidence while we reach out to the person in need with compassion and action. When the string is tight, the power flows. When we are disengaged or uncaring on either end, the slack in our string dispels the anointing before it can reach the needy person.

It is so easy to allow the anointing to flow through your life. We live in a world where no one seems to care about anyone, so all we have to do is to be caring and compassionate. Compassion is the trigger that releases the anointing. When you are faced with an opportunity, just stop and ask that person how he or she is doing. They will most often respond, "Fine, thank you." You may have to ask a second time, "Seriously, how are you doing today?" If you compassionately press in, you will get a response. I have found this catches people off guard, and many times they will eventually pour out a few of their struggles or needs. Then all you have to do is lovingly pray for them. Reach as far as you can up toward God and as far out as you can with compassion toward them. The anointing wants to flow, but we must usually create the moment.

The anointing wants to flow, but we must usually create the moment.

A little while ago, I was in an electronics store, looking for a specific repair part. As I found my way to the back of the empty store, I began to dig into a large discount bin of parts. While I was digging around, a man walked up behind me. He was staring at radios, and when I turned around and said, "Hello," I noticed he was rather elderly. He asked me what I was looking for, and I mentioned the specific electronic part I was looking for. He looked at me wide eyed and to my surprise he said, "When I was detained in a German prisoner of war camp during World War II, some buddies and I made a crystal radio with a few parts like what you are looking for. We used a bedspring and a piece of wire to tune in the frequency of the BBC so we could get the news from the Allies!"

I was overwhelmed at his courage and ingenuity; he was a true hero. He went on to say, "That's all I want to buy today, just a radio."

I thanked him for his brave service to our nation, then asked him if he was doing alright.

He responded, "No, not really. My wife is in the final stages of Lou Gehrig's Disease. She probably only has a day or two left; she is under Hospice care. We have really enjoyed an AM radio station over the years that plays big band music from the 1940's—when we met. Today our radio died and I know she really likes the music playing all day long in the background. I just want her to be comfortable when she goes."

I offered to go and pray for her, but he kindly refused, "No, it is her time to meet God; she is a Christian."

I asked the man if he was serving the Lord, to which he replied, "I used to." At this point, tears filled his eyes and spilled over, running down his cheeks. It was so easy and natural to pray for him in that moment. The "string" was tight, and the anointing flowed so naturally.

After prayer, as he was leaving, he told me, "My wife is going to be so happy knowing that I've made my peace with God."

Proclaiming the good news to the broken is the main reason why Jesus sends the Dove upon us. We are called to be compassionate representatives of the Anointed One, fulfilling His continued mission and not pretending to be some religious Elvis impersonator looking for attention.

Now let us shift our attention to being spiritually sensitive and cultivating this anointing of power in our lives.

"I owe everything to the gift of Pentecost."

Samuel Chadwick

"A church in the land without the Spirit is rather a curse than a blessing. If you have not the Spirit of God, Christian worker, remember that you stand in somebody else's way; you are a fruitless tree standing where a fruitful tree might grow."

Charles Spurgeon

Reflection questions:

1. Can you think of anyone in the Old Testament whom the Jews may have suspected to be the Messiah?

2. In what ways did Jesus fulfill the prophecies about the Messiah?

3. How does the Holy Spirit's power help us to continue the mission of Jesus?

Goodbye Chicken • Hello Dove

Part Three:

How to Use the Holy Spirit's Power

Goodbye Chicken • Hello Dove

Chapter Seven
Atmospheres and Appetites

I do not claim to be some mighty prophet or apostle, nor have I been beamed up to the mothership or seen the images of saints appear on a toasted bagel. I do, however, understand from Scripture that it is natural for believers who walk with God to hear the Spirit's voice. Hearing His voice is supposed to be an outgrowth of being the temple of the Holy Spirit (1 Cor 3:16; 6:19), but how can we improve our ability to hear His voice? This was exactly the question I recently asked Him. But first, let me tell you about someone who encouraged me in my quest to follow the Spirit.

Smith Wigglesworth (1859-1947) was a British plumber who moonlighted as a powerful Pentecostal healing evangelist. I first read a book of his transcribed sermons entitled *Ever Increasing Faith*. I was about fifteen years old and was drawn to this book because I desired to learn all I could about the Holy Spirit and His power. Wigglesworth was well qualified to speak on the subject because the historical account of his ministry reads like the book of Acts with healings, divine revelations, exorcisms, Spirit baptisms and even raising several people from the dead. That book stirred such an intense hunger in my life for the Holy Spirit's ministry. Afterward, I experienced new promptings from the Spirit and began to act upon them.

As I stepped out, trying to be obedient in this new realm of spiritual experiences, I encountered a confusing mix of success and failure. Because of this, I had so many questions, but I was too timid to ask others, especially about my failures. So, one day I decided to ask the Holy Spirit Himself. Surprisingly, He answered, and I learned one of the most beneficial lessons of my spiritual life: ask Him. What benefit is it for us to have the Holy Spirit available as our Teacher if we never show up to class?

What benefit is it for us to have the Holy Spirit available as our Teacher if we never show up to class?

Again, it is natural to hear His voice, if we tune in. This is why I love to ask the Spirit as many questions as I can. I do not always get an answer, but when I do it is so incredibly helpful. Recently in my prayer life, I asked the Holy Spirit if there was a way to improve my ability to hear His voice more clearly and stay more focused. To my surprise, I sensed an answer from a gentle whisper inside: "atmospheres and appetites." That was it, two words and no explanation. I quickly wrote those two words down and began to look for their meaning. I adjusted my radar on these two words to see what I would pick up during my prayer and Bible reading. As time has passed, I have found that these words have become incredibly important, simplifying and transformational in my ability to hear His voice. I pray that you will value them by the end of this chapter as well.

Atmospheres

The Bible speaks often about our surroundings, not merely geographical ones but relational and circumstantial surroundings. These relational and circumstantial environments can be both intentional surroundings (choosing with whom, when and where I spend time) and unintentional ones (allowing my life environments to simply happen with no forethought). From the original perfection of the Garden of Eden—where before sin, man communed with God in the cool of the day—to the lonely, anguishing communion of the Garden of Gethsemane, intentional positioning has had incredible benefit. Conversely, unintentional atmospheres can lead to a world of pain; just ask battle-fatigued King David whose casual rooftop stroll started a chain reaction of sin, culminating in murder. I have learned a life-changing principle about atmospheres that has dramatically improved the way I hear the Spirit's voice.

I must intentionally choose my atmospheres; if not, I will automatically, by default, find myself in negative, unintentional ones. Our living environment may be negative, with a bad neighborhood, school or workplace. Perhaps you mingle with the wrong crowd—even at your church. Though we may not always be able to change the circumstances of our environment, we can choose our atmosphere because the atmospheres I am referring to are in our mind and spirit.

Emotional/Mental Atmospheres

Have you ever been around someone going through terrible times and yet they are seemingly filled with joy? When we were first married, my wife, Rochelle, and I used to visit an elderly lady named Bea. She had recently lost her husband, Les, after about sixty years of marriage. Even though he had advanced Parkinson's disease and had not been able to walk or speak for years, Bea kept Les at home, caring for him as a compassionate nurse and adoring wife. They did not have many material possessions and had persistent, overwhelming medical bills. She was nearly blind and could only read with a massive, brightly-lit magnifying glass that was mounted to a floor stand. Her environment was not ideal by any means, but Bea understood the power of choosing the right emotional/mental atmosphere.

> *I must intentionally choose my atmospheres; if not, I will automatically, by default, find myself in negative, unintentional ones.*

The first time we visited her was to "encourage her," but the next visits became lessons on how to find the goodness of God amidst incredibly negative circumstances. Within just a few minutes of entering Bea's small apartment, her contagious smile and laughter would get ahold of us. She would talk about how good God had been to her and Les, enabling them to be together so long, and how good God was to take Les home when his health had finally failed. She would smile as she talked about dancing with Les again in heaven. We would always pray together before departing, and we would leave feeling better than when we had entered because of Bea's choice to be positive. She never denied or ignored the negative, but simply chose to "accentuate the positive," and she constantly and accurately represented God's love to her neighbors. Bea carefully guarded her emotional/mental atmosphere because she understood how powerful and yet fragile it could be.

You may wonder how this relates to hearing the Ho_y Spirit's voice, so let me explain. I have heard many people say things like, "My life is terrible," or, "I have missed all my opportunities" or, "I can never do anything great for God," or, "Why can everyone else hear God's voice but me?" While these statements may accurately express a person's *feelings*, they may not accurately express *God's reality*. For some reason, humans tend to unquestionably trust their internal feelings about something over what others, even what the Word of God, says. Our feelings at any given moment could very well be an incorrect reflection of our broken human nature. Though we all will face challenges, God has designed our lives to experience fulfillment through those challenges. He has built each one of us to do something meaningful, and through that process, every Christian is designed to hear His voice. Instead of wasting moments during my limited time span by reinforcing and rehearsing my deficiencies and disappointments, why not use the time constructively in prayer, welcoming God's miracles? If your GPS coordinates are set to "I will never hear His voice," that will likely be your destination; you are closing doors in your life. If your coordinates are set to "Lord, teach me to hear Your voice. I know it is Your will," this will be your destination. Prayer welcomes divine help. Complaining welcomes trouble or, worse yet, the fellowship of other complainers.

Wigglesworth said,

> If we have our consciousness filled with the presence of the glory of the Lord, there will be no room even for the aggressive errors of destructive criticism, or for bitter disappoint-

ment…If we keep evil out of that inner realm, we destroy its virulence.[8]

I am not advocating denying your circumstances or some sort of mind-over-matter technique. I am, however, encouraging you to spend your energy on something that builds up rather than something that pulls down. Emotional and mental atmospheres are important, but the most important atmosphere is in the spiritual realm.

Spiritual Atmospheres

Unlike emotional or mental atmospheres that are operating primarily in the natural realm, spiritual atmospheres are just that, spiritual. We are no longer trying to call ourselves to a higher place; we are trying to be better hosts of the Holy Spirit who lives within us, so that His ministry calls us to a higher place.

Regarding these spiritual atmospheres, the word *input* has become very important to me. I have learned that the input I either allow or disallow into my life dramatically affects my spiritual outcome. For example, if I fill my life with argumentative, angry political podcasts, radio and television programs, I find I am more argumentative. If I watch or listen to media that is full of things that are not beneficial, I find those thoughts fill my mind and distract me from where I should have my focus. Whatever we feed will grow; whatever we sow, that is what we reap. That works for both negative and, thankfully, positive input. I have found that something as simple as worship music quietly playing in the

[8] Frodsham, Stanley H. *Smith Wigglesworth Apostle of Faith*. 1st ed. Springfield, MO: Gospel Publishing House, 1949. Print (123).

background can enable me to experience God's peace. Or, the commitment that I made years ago, that I would pray and worship while I am getting ready each morning. That commitment made a significant difference in the spiritual atmosphere surrounding me throughout the day.

But here is where the Spirit has been recently challenging me again in this area of atmospheres. The more I intentionally stop during the day and put out the welcome mat for Him, the more He reveals Himself to me. In other words, He rewards extra effort toward Him. Or, as the Bible says, "He rewards those who diligently seek Him" (Hebrews 11:6). Creating a positive atmosphere, where I can experience God and hear His voice, should be an intentional act, not a passive one. It's not that difficult. Just stop for a moment and welcome Him. I dare you to try it right now!

Recently, I had a rather stressful chain of events unexpectedly come my way. I found myself frustrated, sitting and trying to relive the circumstance over and over. That response was not necessarily wrong or sinful, but it was not perhaps the most beneficial. Realizing this, I shut the door of my office, raised my hands to heaven and began to worship and pray in tongues. Within just a few moments, God's presence moved over me and restored my peace. I knew everything was going to be alright. He rewards extra effort. Environment is our circumstance, but intentional atmospheres are set by our choice to minimize negative or destructive thinking and maximize Godward pursuit. As we intentionally guard our minds and spirits, we find healthier desires emerging and will naturally hear the Spirit's voice.

The issue of intentionally setting a mental/emotional or spiritual atmosphere connects to addition and subtraction— subtracting some negatives and adding some positives. Subtract destructive thinking and thoughts that lead to temptation while adding, in their place, promises from Scripture and prayerful, worshipful priorities. The more you cultivate a healthy mental/emotional and spiritual atmosphere, the more your intimacy with God will grow. The atmospheres we choose will dramatically affect our spiritual appetites, affecting how well we hear the Holy Spirit.

> Fix your thoughts on what is true, and honorable, and right, and pure, and lovely, and admirable. Think about things that are excellent and worthy of praise (Philippians 4:8).

Appetites

I do not know about you, but there are a few foods that I will avoid with my strongest effort. Since my earliest childhood, I have possessed a strong aversion to liver and onions. This satanic marriage summons a strong gag reflex. There is nothing about liver and onions that is desirable for me: texture, flavor or stench. (I am sorry; stench was unkind. I meant to say, "vile, despicable odor.") The fact that it is organ "meat" certainly does not help its cause. Liver's evil superpower is so strong that it can even pollute the usually versatile and harmless onion, converting it into a pawn of gastroenterological abomination. I am not really sure if I am communicating my disdain clearly enough.

Conversely, there are some foods I love and would eat without question. Take chocolate, for instance. To me, if liver is the filthy bus stop to digestive perdition, chocolate may be the portal to culinary nirvana. Or, what about barbeque…anything? Except liver. My point is that we all have appetites for certain foods, while others we find unappetizing.

If you choose to allow your final health and wellness goals to determine your choice of foods, you will have a considerably different diet from one dictated by your temporary whims and moods. If you want to live long and minimize as many health risks as possible, you may wish to skip donuts—forever. However, if you are given to impulse, maybe a dozen or two would hit the spot. One appetite is controlled by long term goals; the other is dominated by immediate gratification. One leads to a preferred outcome; the other to the most risky, dubious, likely undesirable destination. Spiritual appetites have many correlations to natural appetites. If you focus on your final desired outcome at your starting point, your choices now will be significantly different. If you are driven by impulse and sugar addiction, good luck on ever hitting your spiritual goals.

If you focus on your final desired outcome at your starting point, your choices now will be significantly different.

When I first read the Wigglesworth sermon book, a lofty appetite stirred me; I wanted to attempt becoming a great man of God in my lifetime. Wigglesworth was eighty-eight years old when he passed away. During his life, he was often a walking representation of Jesus. He certainly had human flaws and weaknesses, but the spiritual characteristics far outlasted the human ones. Though I have certainly not arrived at my ideal, by any means, I am further down the road now because of feeding my healthy appetites and starving unhealthy ones.

Speaking of spiritual appetites and starving, I went on my first forty day fast while studying at Central Bible College in Springfield, Missouri. My close friend, and later brother-in-law,

Shane Wilson and I were increasingly challenging each other to go deeper in the things of the Holy Spirit. We sat up late one night and passionately discussed becoming mighty men of God. We were convinced that the only way to attain that goal was by an immediate forty-day fast. We started that next morning with a season of powerful prayer and worship, then went to classes. After going to the dorm's prayer room during lunch, we both needed to run some errands and decided to go together. As we drove through downtown Springfield, we passed a hole-in-the-wall restaurant named Hamby's; it was a local favorite. Neither Shane nor I had ever eaten there before, so there was no overpowering taste bud memory at work, but nonetheless we were both overwhelmed with temptation to eat. I was driving and the steering wheel just wanted to aim into the rarely-open parking space right by the busy restaurant's front door. I parked and turned the car off. Shane asked me what I was doing, to which I replied, "I heard they have great pie." With that, we were out of the car, sitting in a booth and guiltily taking the tiny first bite of the juiciest cheeseburger we had eaten since beginning our forty-day fast. To say we were overwhelmed with personal disappointment and guilt would be an understatement, but one bite led to another, and then to a piece of pie. And "they" were right; the pie was exceptional. It was over. Our radical forty-day fast was condensed into a mere sixteen hours. I bet even Smith Wigglesworth could not do that. Can you identify with my struggle between strong spiritual desires and weak implementation?

There is a growth curve involved in cultivating spiritual appetites. A complete forty-day fast may not be the most achievable goal to aim for at first when that spiritual appetite is not developed. Why not start with a day or two? This is what I learned from the failure celebration dinner at Hamby's. I needed to allow my appetites to grow, and not for pie, by the way. My next fast was three days, and it was not sidelined by burgers and pie, thank God. The next fast was a week.

One of the most significant, long-term revelations for me has been the interrelation between atmospheres and appetites. Atmospheres affect our appetites. Just like the events leading to my first forty day fast, I have found that getting around people who have the same spiritual desires has a way of stirring me to a higher level of commitment and consistency. However, I have also found that controlling other atmospheres (like not even slowing down while driving past Hamby's) enables those good intentions to become reality.

Can you identify with my struggle between strong spiritual desires and weak implementation?

Three Important Spiritual Appetites

Here are the three primary appetites you need to cultivate so you can have greater clarity in hearing the Holy Spirit's voice. Disclaimer: You will not be surprised by the first two.

Prayer is a primary appetite that we need to cultivate. I am not referring to some sort of religious bondage to prayer created by guilt, but prayer itself. It is not difficult to see how simply talking with someone allows you to know him more and recognize his voice more easily. Have you ever received a phone call and the caller ID was not working? If you choose to answer, the game of guessing who it is begins. You say to yourself, "It kind of sounds like Aunt Marge, but with a chest cold." If it was someone you spoke to frequently, voice recognition would be no problem. The more we pray, the more easily we recognize the Holy Spirit's voice.

Some people are in an artificial bondage to praying for a specific, currently unachievable length of time, so they choose to not pray at all. Their spiritual appetite has not yet been developed to pray for an hour, so instead of praying at all, they wallow in guilt and prayerlessness. Wigglesworth was well known for saying, "I don't very often spend more than a half hour in prayer at one time, but I never go more than a half hour without praying."[9] Prayer does not have to be viewed like you are handwriting a twenty-page letter. Why not view it as an all-day text thread? Start somewhere and allow your prayer appetite to develop.

The second primary appetite is the Word of God. Reading it; speaking it; memorizing it; assimilating it. The Bible is the will and way of God, and there is no other path to knowing His will and way aside from His Word. Every time you read the Bible, you are hearing the Holy Spirit's voice. In fact, you can hear the "audible" voice of God anytime you read the Word out loud.

Have you ever wondered if an impression you have received is from God or if it is only human imagination? There is a Scripture for that problem:

> For the word of God is alive and powerful. It is sharper than the sharpest two-edged sword, cutting between soul and spirit, between joint and marrow. It exposes our innermost thoughts and desires (Hebrews 4:12).

---

[9] Hibbert, Albert. *Smith Wigglesworth: The Secret of His Power.* Tulsa, OK: Harrison House, 1982. Print (41).

Only the Word can discern between soul (human-influenced) and Spirit (God-influenced) realms. Someone who refuses to read the Word consistently will always struggle to hear the Holy Spirit's voice. They lack power to distinguish between their voice, the voice of others and the voice of the Spirit.

Smith Wigglesworth learned how to read later in life, as an adult, under his wife Polly's instruction. Because his main passion was knowing God, he chose to devote his new skill to reading only God's book. He was often quoted as saying, "I have never read any book but the Bible." [10] Lester Sumrall remembered that Smith would not allow him to bring a newspaper into the Wigglesworth residence in Bradford, England. [11] That may be a bit extreme, but I do understand where he was coming from—prioritizing God's Word. The fruit of his immovable decision to honor the Scriptures was consistently hearing the Spirit's voice.

Someone who refuses to consistently read the Word will always struggle in hearing the Holy Spirit's voice.

The final primary appetite is self-denial or consecration. I bet you wish I had said naps and eating at buffet restaurants. Me too. No one naturally enjoys denying their fleshly appetites, but probably everyone would like the personal benefits that come with self-discipline. Self-denial is not some sort of self-imposed misery that causes us discomfort and thereby makes God "happy" in some dark, ironic way. Self-denial is what Jesus commanded:

---

[10] Frodsham, 109.
[11] Sumrall, Lester. *Pioneers of Faith*. Tulsa, OK: Harrison House, 1995. Print (161-162).

> Then Jesus said to His disciples, "If anyone
> wishes to come after Me, he must deny
> himself, and take up his cross and follow Me
> (Matthew 16:24).

Self-denial is the behavior associated with self-control. Self-denial enables us to recognize and reduce needless clutter that drains our brains and clutters our spirits, resulting in significantly greater clarity. Remember Hamby's pie? It was remarkable, but it was also a sign to me that my flesh's appetite was stronger than my spirit's desires. After my colossal failure, I began to take more manageable bites of self-denial with much greater success. Fasting food is not the only form of self-denial. Many years ago, Rochelle and I decided that any movie or TV show that blasphemes the name of Jesus is not worthy of our time. As an area of consecration, we shut it off, no questions or appeals. Jesus is far too precious for us to allow His name to be ridiculed for our entertainment; we do not want to join the crowd mocking Him. This principle subtracts a lot of potential movies for us, but we are not sad about it. This small area of self-denial reaps the benefit of a clearer ability to hear the Spirit's voice. Perhaps you are "addicted" to social media, shopping, outdoor sports, etc. Perhaps you may wish to set them aside for a short while and let your fleshly hunger submit to your spiritual hunger. Perhaps you may wish to evaluate the time, effort and resources spent on these areas and place some limits on them. I have a friend who refuses to order a large-sized portion of any food or drink, simply as an outworking of self-denial and moderation. Any area of imbalance in fleshly appetite could use some consecration.

The atmospheres we choose dramatically affect our spiritual appetites because the two work in tandem. We begin to establish new atmospheres by doing what we know someone with healthy spiritual appetites would do. We press into the Word, dive into prayer and practice self-denial. No matter what we may or may not

Self-denial is the behavior associated with self-control.

feel, we push ourselves closer to God. There is no other way to build spiritual intimacy with God besides spending personal time in the Word, prayer and consecration. There are no shortcuts. Trust me. I have tried them all. They are not faster, but rather long, needless detours that take you back to the same starting point. Someone who prays, reads the Word with consistency and denies his or her flesh knows the Holy Spirit's voice better than someone who does not. It is that simple. Though it is a process, atmospheres help determine appetites and appetites help inaugurate atmospheres. As the Dove's voice becomes clearer, the chicken's voice becomes more insignificant.

"When asceticism becomes a thing of form enforced by man-made rules, it is incapable of dealing with bodily lusts. Self-control on the other hand is the fruit of the Spirit, springing from divine life within, cultivated by the habit of a disciplined life."

Arthur Wallace

Goodbye Chicken • Hello Dove

"A full measure of the Word and prayer each day gives a healthy and powerful life."

Andrew Murray

Reflection questions:

1. Can you think of some personal examples where a negative atmosphere affected you in a negative way?

2. Can you think of some personal examples where a positive atmosphere affected you in a positive way?

3. Are there any ways that you consistently implement self-denial in your life? What would be a small step you could try to take in this direction?

Chapter Eight
Following the Dove

Have you ever awakened on a sunny morning, gotten out of bed and opened the curtains? Suddenly the room was flooded with brilliant, warm light. Most likely, your eyes squinted for a few moments until you adjusted to the sudden burst of a welcoming radiance filling the room. Sunlight has a positive effect on nearly everything: it shines, it brings light, warmth, photosynthesis, solar power, etc. However, most people do not stop to contemplate a big problem with sunlight—it reveals how things really are.

Before you opened the curtains in your room, you were likely satisfied with your air quality. But after opening the drapes, that filthy sunlight dragged in all sorts of visible dust particles now floating everywhere in the air.

Actually, that is not how it works. The dust particles were already there. In fact, whether you see them or not, they are floating all around us now (sorry germaphobes).

If we could open our spiritual drapes, letting the proper illumination envelope us, we would see just how much activity of the Holy Spirit is around us. We are often like the dull-eyed servant of Elisha who could not believe what he could not see:

When the servant of the man of God got up early the next morning and went outside, there were troops, horses, and chariots everywhere. "Oh, sir, what will we do now?" the young man cried to Elisha. "Don't be afraid!" Elisha told him. "For there are more on our side than on theirs!" Then Elisha prayed, "O LORD, open his eyes and let him see!" The LORD opened the young man's eyes, and when he looked up, he saw that the hillside around Elisha was filled with horses and chariots of fire (2 Kings 6:15-17).

How many times have we missed the Spirit's leading because our eyes have grown accustomed to our sense-darkened, infrequent expectations of the moving of the Spirit? But how often does the Spirit desire to move powerfully?

Many years ago, I was preaching at a church in one of the coastal areas of Canada. Before the first service began, a kind, elderly gentleman approached me and said, "You will like it here; we are a V-E-R-Y Spirit-filled church." He emphasized the word "very" by drawing it out for a very long time.

My curiosity was stirred, so I asked him, "What does a V-E-R-Y Spirit-filled church' mean to you?"

He replied, "Well we hardly go a month without at least one tongues with interpretation in our church services."

His definition was essentially that the expectation of the Spirit's moving was "few and far between." Unfortunately, this low anticipation is common among believers. It is hard to clearly see what is all around us when fear, religious traditions, bad doctrine or Spirit-quenching has sewn the curtains shut. Everyone inside the room is squinting spiritually but no longer realizes it because, unfortunately, it has become a way of life.

What does the Bible say about how frequently we should expect the moving of the Holy Spirit in our personal lives and churches? Do you remember some of the biblical types and symbols of the Spirit discussed in chapter two? All of them relate to the Spirit's movement and activity, not dormant inactivity. The wind blows, the oil pours, the water flows, the fire burns, the dove descends. The Holy Spirit is always moving, even when our spiritual environment is too dark to perceive Him. He is always there and always moving. Always!

When religious leaders harassed Jesus for healing on the Sabbath when He "should have been" resting, He replied, "My Father is always working and so am I" (John 5:17). If the Father and Son are always working, how could the Spirit be on vacation? From the first reference in Genesis of the Holy Spirit

The Holy Spirit is always moving, even when our spiritual environment is too dark to perceive Him.

"moving over the waters" (Gen 1:2) to the last in Revelation where He is speaking (Rev 22:17), He is always moving, speaking, empowering, transforming, purifying. He is not lazy nor is He resting up for His next big gig. He has never changed His ways.

We grasp the basic principle that the Holy Spirit is always moving, and yet we seldom prepare for or count on Him moving anywhere near us. I have often wondered how many lost persons He is convicting, sick He is healing, Christians He is anointing or gifts He is stirring at any one moment on planet earth. And He is especially busy on the fourth Sunday of the month in coastal Canada.

In the first chapter, we talked about the Wizard of Pride hiding behind a curtain of fear. But now, after walking through Scripture and seeing God's plan for us all, why would we ever want to live with bare-minimum, lowest-common-denominator, fear-based, chicken-coddling inactivity? God desires to use all of us for His glory, but we are afraid, under educated, under resourced, under motivated; basically, "under" everything. So, after we are saved, He wants to baptize us in His Holy Spirit, giving us access to heaven's courage, heaven's wisdom, heaven's guidance, heaven's resources and heaven's power. He puts this treasure in earthen vessels to show that the power comes from Him and not from us (1 Corinthians 4:9). It is now time to open that curtain of fear and let the light shine! All around us are floating miracles, prophetic words, demonstrations of power and so much more. The atmosphere surrounding a Spirit-filled, consecrated Christian is alive with supernatural possibility!

Over the years, I have met many who have been legitimately baptized in the Holy Spirit, but do not know what to do afterwards, aside from praying in tongues. Remember, praying in tongues is wonderful and certainly builds us up (Jude 1:20), but it is not the point. The point is the confidence and bravery, that the One who prompts us to speak in tongues will now prompt us to speak to others. Just as Spirit-filled Christians can pray in tongues whenever they yield to the Spirit, they can now supernaturally minister to others whenever yielded to the same Spirit, because He is always moving. The Dove brings confidence, bravery and power to override our natural, chicken-like inclinations.

Six Principles to Recognize the Spirit's Leading More Clearly

How can we more clearly perceive the Dove's leading and follow Him into this supernatural possibility? Over the years I have journaled about six principles that have significantly helped me on the journey to follow the Dove.

1. It grows through relationship and spiritual intimacy.

In the last chapter, we focused on appetites and atmospheres, a parallel concept to this principle. Let me give even greater focus and perspective to this truth. Knowing God better means that you naturally know His voice better. However, it is the natural inclination of humanity to try to find an easier way of doing things than investing in long-term relationship. I am subject to that same inclination.

In the late 1940s to the mid 1960s, there was a large supernatural revival movement in America; historians call it the *Post World War II Salvation/Healing Revival*. This revival was a grassroots, non-denominational movement led by evangelists who operated in powerful signs and wonders ministries. Notable participants were Oral Roberts, William Branham, William Freeman, Jack Coe, Sr., A. A. Allen, T. L. Osborn, Tommy Hicks, Louise Nankivell, Gayle Jackson and a host of others. Because there was no apostolic or denominational structure to hold these men and women accountable to a doctrinal or ethical standard, there were some rather tragic and public moments of failure and division. Through some divinely-orchestrated events, an Assemblies of God pastor from the Pacific Northwest, Gordon Lindsay, found himself in the middle of the revival as a respected leader among the evangelists. The magazine he founded, *The Voice of Healing*, became the primary gathering point for the hungry masses as well as providing a much needed organizational and apostolic covering for the participating evangelists.

If you wanted your evangelistic ministry to associate with *The Voice of Healing*, you had to have a proven ministry, adhere to an ethical agreement, agree to a lenient doctrinal code and agree to work interdenominationally. Gordon Lindsay was a true man of God and carried the burden of rallying a tribe of fiercely independent evangelists to the common goal of winning souls. As evidence of his commitment to people coming to Christ, his organization would later change its name to Christ for the Nations, headquartered in Dallas. It is still a powerful global force in training young people for the ministry.

The *Voice of Healing* magazine would often feature autobiographical articles written by one of the nearly 200 participating evangelists. These articles would tell of God's dealings and how the gift of healing began to operate in their lives. Since God had profoundly affected my life through the ministry of Smith Wigglesworth, finding long-out-of-print issues of *The Voice of Healing* was like striking gold. The testimonies of miracles and the personal stories of these anointed evangelists were deeply moving and encouraging. However, an unexpected, reoccurring problem began to stand out to me.

Very frequently, the evangelists would offer instructions on how to receive healing, but curiously and just as frequently, their methods would totally contradict each other! How could this be? In spite of their differences, they ended up with the same result. They got to the same outcome, in spite of radically different processes. One would prescribe a fast of a certain amount of days, while another would demand attendance to a certain amount of his or her evangelistic services. One would demand a "positive state of mind," while another would condemn that practice as "Mind Science." Despite contradictory instructions, they saw the same level of persuasive healings. This discrepancy really bothered me until I stepped back and saw the bigger picture. Perhaps the different, contradictory instructions the evangelists thought were contributing to their healing ministries were not actually behind the results at all. Perhaps the answer was much simpler. I had noticed a trend in the different evangelists' personal testimonies about "how the gift came" to each of them. Each one had devoted extra personal time to fasting, the Word and prayer. Some went as far as going to the woods alone for a few weeks. One of them, who struggled with self-discipline, famously had his wife lock him in a closet so he could fast and pray! Each one of these men and women had pressed into deeper levels of personal intimacy and relationship with the Holy Spirit through feeding the three primary spiritual appetites outlined in the last chapter: prayer, reading the Word and self-denial. Satisfying these three appetites is essential to deepening your relationship, and therefore, bringing spiritual authority and power into your life. There are no easy shortcuts. More relationship = better spiritual hearing = more Holy Spirit activity. Jesus said,

> If you abide in Me, and My words abide in
> you, ask whatever you wish, and it will be
> done for you (John 15:7 NASB).

2. It must line up with the Word and mission of Jesus.

This is obvious: The Spirit will not lead you to do something contrary to the Word of God or the mission of Jesus.

The Holy Spirit's voice and power flow in the direction they have always moved—toward Jesus.

Some time ago, I heard a terrible story of how an apparently spiritual man nearly destroyed a church, blaming it on the Holy Spirit's leading. This man had previously been in church leadership and had been used in public prophecy to some extent. When a new pastor came, this man cornered the pastor and demanded that specific changes be made to the church. When the pastor graciously said he would prayerfully consider the changes, the man became incensed. He began to interrupt the services by shouting publicly condemning prophecies that accused the new pastor of being hard-hearted and even engaged in secret sin. Because of the integrity of the pastor, the church elders stood with the pastor, attempted to discipline the man and forbade any future outbursts, but the man would not stop. He would secretly contact other church members and tell them of dreams and visions he had regarding the sin of the pastor. Finally, the leadership had to dis-fellowship the man from the church, but the damage had already been done. His apparent spiritual gifts had cast a shadow of doubt over the existing leadership, and the church was deeply divided. I bet you can figure out what happened next. The man went and started his own church with the people he had manipulated to leave. Unfortunately, the existing church was cut in half.

The Holy Spirit's voice and power flow in the direction they have always moved— toward Jesus.

A decade later, the pastor who had been wrongfully accused was still faithfully pastoring his rebuilt congregation, but the false prophet had a terrible fall, deeply injuring those he had led astray. The Holy Spirit had not spoken to this man to destroy the church; it was the man's own evil, covetous desire to have his own way, resulting in the destruction of the church. The revelation of secret sins for which he was blaming the pastor were really his own. This was not a church plant; it was a pillaging of God's family. The Holy Spirit will never lead anyone to destroy the mission of Jesus. The promptings and voice of the Spirit are in line with Scripture. This is another reason why we should grow in the Word!

3. It is often quieter and less spectacular than anticipated.

In our world of smoke and lights, pyrotechnics and special effects, it is only normal for us to expect something as supernatural as the Holy Spirit's voice to be loud and spectacular. However, Elijah's encounter on Mt. Sinai challenges that assumption.

> And as Elijah stood there, the LORD passed by, and a mighty windstorm hit the mountain. It was such a terrible blast that the rocks were torn loose, but the LORD was not in the wind. After the wind there was an earthquake, but the LORD was not in the earthquake. And after the earthquake there was a fire, but the LORD was not in the fire. And after the fire there was the sound of a gentle whisper. When Elijah heard it, he wrapped his face in his cloak and went out and stood at the entrance of the cave (1 Kings 19:11-13).

153

If the great God of the cosmos was speaking, surely, He would have utilized all His otherworldly resources, or at least a windstorm, earthquake or firestorm. However, Elijah discovered that he needed to hear beyond the loud, spectacular noises to find the gentle whispers of the Spirit. When Elijah recognized the subtle nudge, he reverently wrapped his face in his cloak and stepped out to approach God. In the same way, we must not only be looking to the sky for massive signs in the heavens, but must learn to hear the gentle promptings from the Holy Spirit. This is a common way He leads us.

One time I was leaving a church service, and I passed a woman still sitting in her seat quietly praying. The smallest inner nudge from the Holy Spirit came to me. I sensed that He wanted to heal her. It was so small, barely perceivable, that any less would have been unnoticeable to me. Trusting the way I have learned the Spirit speaks to me, I stopped and asked her if I could pray for her about something. She expressed her need for healing, but before I could even pray, she began to smile, cry and joyfully whisper, "I'm healed! The pain just left!" I do not ever want to miss His gentle nudges.

Though God could send fireworks, He often gently nudges us. Personally, I would estimate that the majority of the times I have sensed His leading or prompting it has been a gentle whisper, not a loud or spectacular sign.

4. It is never based on 100% intellectual certainty.

Remember that we are dealing with a supernatural prompting, not a natural one. We are not looking to our natural senses or understanding to validate the prompting. Let me illustrate.

For over two years I prayed to be baptized in the Holy Spirit. I know now that there was never a wasted moment in the seeking process, but at that time, I had grown rather frustrated and discouraged. The same pattern of pressing into God's presence, then feeling the Holy Spirit beginning to stir me, had happened many times. When I had sensed His stirring and presence each time, a few funny-sounding syllables had begun to float through my conscious awareness. I would always dismiss them as just my imagination and tried to put them out of my mind. On the night I finally began to speak in a supernatural language, this same pattern had occurred again. However, this time I was so frustrated I decided to quit seeking ever again. As I began to wind down my prayer time by thanking the Lord, I suddenly felt the Holy Spirit's presence was stirring again. And guess what? The same funny syllables began to come to my awareness. All of a sudden, I did the math; those funny words never crossed my mind when I was anywhere but desperately seeking to be filled with the Holy Spirit and when His presence was noticeably stirring me. I remember whispering, "Jesus, have you been trying to get me to say those words all along?" I never heard an angel choir sing a resounding "Yes!" but I was suddenly filled with just enough courage to try saying the syllables out loud, which I did. The moment I began to speak them, I experienced a wonderful inner release of God's power. I was speaking in tongues quietly, my spirit was praying, but my intellect was not particularly impressed.

The promptings of the Spirit do not come from our brain; they come from the Holy Spirit and flow to our spirit. Our intellect cannot fully understand them and often does not like them because they are not intellectually based.

For His Spirit searches out everything and shows us God's deep secrets. No one can know a person's thoughts except that person's own spirit, and no one can know God's thoughts except God's own Spirit. And we have received God's Spirit (not the world's spirit), so we can know the wonderful things God has freely given us (1 Corinthians 2:10-12).

> *We may have spiritual certainty, yet at the same time, have considerable intellectual concerns.*

We may have spiritual certainty, yet at the same time have considerable intellectual concerns. The natural mind is only comfortable when relying on what our natural skills and ability can achieve. The Spirit's promptings are often for us to step out into unknown territory; no wonder we experience intellectual concern. The more we learn how the Holy Spirit speaks to us, the more confidently we can follow.

5. **It is a developing process.**

Have you ever used a Polaroid camera to take an instant picture and then watched it develop? (Sorry, for those who have no idea what a Polaroid camera is; it is an old technology that has both camera and printer incorporated into the camera body.) When the camera spits out the white-bordered print, the photo area is a solid gray. Slowly, dark outlines begin to emerge, as shapes in the photo become visible. Then, dull colors begin to appear and grow in their vividness. And finally, the picture brightens, fully developed.

As a kid, I remember being in a church service where an evangelist was used in revelatory, prophetic ministry. I was so afraid he would point me out publicly and announce my sins or reveal that I had gotten mad at my sisters and hidden their dolls in the back of the closet for revenge. I just assumed that people who heard from God knew everything about everyone, like they had hacked God's hard drive and had complete access to all His files. This is not the case. As Scripture so plainly says, "No one can know a person's thoughts except that person's own spirit, and no one can know God's thoughts except God's own Spirit" (1 Corinthians 2:11). Even the greatest prophets in the Old Testament only knew the things God revealed to them. Only Jesus has the Spirit without measure; only His divine Polaroid camera can instantly develop a picture, while ours take some processing time and have limited content exposure.

The Apostle Paul had a similar developing experience when he heard the Spirit's leading prior to his voyage to Rome:

> Paul began to admonish them, and said to
> them, "Men, I perceive that the voyage will
> certainly be with damage and great loss, not
> only of the cargo and the ship, but also of our
> lives" (Acts 27:10, NASB).

However, after some time had elapsed and he had more time to pray and reflect, greater clarity was given to him:

> Yet now I urge you to keep up your courage,
> for there will be no loss of life among you, but

only of the ship. For this very night an angel
of the God to whom I belong and whom I
serve stood before me, saying, 'Do not be
afraid, Paul; you must stand before Caesar;
and behold, God has granted you all those
who are sailing with you' (Acts 27:22-24,
NASB).

No one was going to lose their lives; however, there was
indeed going to be great loss. Paul's perception of the Spirit's voice
developed over a short period of time.

The House

A few years ago, I was speaking at a Midwestern church.
While praying a general prayer of blessing over a couple, I began
to sense the presence of the Holy Spirit, so I quieted my heart to
listen. In a few moments, some vague, supernatural revelation
started to unfold. I began to see a blurry picture of a house. It came
to me like an old personal memory, but the more I focused on
Jesus, the clearer it became. I did not have empirical intellectual
certainty, but rather an inner faith-confidence associated with the
visual images I was experiencing.

The house was covered in pale green siding that had a faux
woodgrain pressed into it and a grey asphalt shingle roof. The roof
shingles were a unique rounded pattern that had woven,
overlapping corners. I could see the front stoop was painted white
and the house number "16" was in black numbers on a white plaque
beside the white front door. Then the revelation stopped
unfolding. I had no idea what it meant; it seemed rather insignificant to me. It was just a house.

Not knowing what my next step was, I paused to ask the Holy Spirit what to do about this revelation. Then, I felt a gentle leading to share it with the lady. "When I started to pray for you folks, I believe the Spirit showed me something, but I do not really understand why it is significant. I could be totally wrong about this, but after praying about it, I feel enough confidence to share it with you." As I began to describe the house, the woman suddenly erupted in terrible anguish, wailing and in pain. She kept bending over at the waist as she cried intensely. I had no idea what to do next, so I quietly asked for more help from the Holy Spirit. I felt Him leading me to prophesy to her, but I only had the first few words to say. However, when I opened my mouth to say the few words that I had, the rest easily followed, "What happened in this house years ago will never hold you back again. Jesus is setting you free from this painful place right now. You are free to function normally again." With those words, she suddenly became silent and gently collapsed to the floor, overcome by supernatural peace from the Holy Spirit. I still had no idea what had happened in that house or, honestly, what was happening at that moment.

After a few minutes, she sat up and began to explain to me and her fiancé what had happened. The house was the place where a relative had, for years, repeatedly sexually abused her as a child. Her adult life had been marked by a pattern of falling in love, getting engaged and then suddenly breaking the engagement off because of fear of sexual contact. She had never told her current fiancé about her private pain and had come for prayer secretly believing God for healing in this area. Supernatural revelation from the Holy Spirit had certainly shown her that God was at work. About a year later, I heard from her and was glad to find out that she was happily married and expecting her first child.

I have discovered over the years that when I perceive the gentle whisper of the Spirit, if I stop and humble myself before the Lord, often the prompting will clarify or develop more if I draw nearer to Jesus in that moment. The Spirit's leadings often flow little by little rather than as a massive download.

6.   It grows with experience.

Finally, I have found that getting some experience under your belt enables you to discern His voice with increasing clarity. There are some lessons that only experience can offer, and when you stay teachable, humble and loving, your mistakes can become positive learning experiences.

I have made so many mistakes over the years! Like the embarrassing time I prayed with a big, burly, flannel-clad lumberjack kind of fellow. This happened during a church service and I had not noticed him in the audience when I was speaking, but when the prayer time was in full swing, I saw him kneeling by the stage with his face buried in his hands and his deep, resonant voice rumbling in prayer. I put my hand on his shoulder and began to pray for him in a general way, "Lord strengthen my brother; raise him up to be a mighty man of God. Empower him to lead other men." As I was praying, I looked down and noticed him turning his head to look at me, exposing the side of his cheek, which had makeup on it. Little dainty earrings were now glistening in the lights. When I saw that obviously feminine face, I wanted to die. It was now very clearly a woman, but her penitent posture and buried face had hidden her identity from me. I was sincerely apologetic, and she was gracious. I am still alive, but I am smarter now.

Not only do we learn from negative experiences, but we can also learn from positive ones. During my later teenage years, I began to have occasional strange sensations in my body when I would pray for people. They were not painful or scary, but I was certainly aware of and sometimes troubled by them. They were the most intense when I would be in some sort of group that was praying. This had gone on for several months, and it was almost becoming a distraction. I remember on one such occasion I had a sensation in one of my knees that felt like a mild vibration. The group was praying, and some were walking around as they prayed. I noticed that the sensation would come and go as I walked around the room. Then I began to realize that it came when I was in a particular area of the room. I walked

I have made so many mistakes over the years! Like the embarrassing time I prayed with…

over to the area and paced around until I found the sensation returning, then took a step away, and it left. It was a very curious phenomenon to me. I stepped forward again, and the vibration returned in my knee; then I stepped backward, and it left. Looking around, I saw that every time I took a step in the direction where the sensation returned, I was nearing a specific person. As I was stepping near him, it happened. I prayed and asked the Holy Spirit, "Am I supposed to pray for that person's knee?" I do not remember getting any answer. As is often the case, there would be no harm in me asking the person if I could pray for him, so this is exactly what I did. And guess what? His knee was the problem, and Jesus was faithful to heal. This sort of learning comes through experience.

Samuel

A great example of this from Scripture is the way the Prophet Samuel grew in his prophetic gifting (1 Sam 3). When he was a young boy—and assisting Eli at the temple—he could not recognize when God audibly called his name on three consecutive occasions. Eli had to assist him to recognize and respond to God calling:

> Now Samuel did not yet know the Lord, nor had the word of the Lord yet been revealed to him. So the Lord called Samuel again for the third time. And he arose and went to Eli and said, "Here I am, for you called me." Then Eli discerned that the Lord was calling the boy. And Eli said to Samuel, "Go lie down, and it shall be if He calls you, that you shall say, 'Speak, Lord, for Your servant is listening.'" So Samuel went and lay down in his place.
>
> Then the Lord came and stood and called as at other times, "Samuel! Samuel!" And Samuel said, "Speak, for Your servant is listening" (1 Samuel 3:7-10).

Fast forward a few years and we read the report of Samuel's growth in discerning the Spirit's voice:

> Thus Samuel grew and the Lord was with him and let none of his words fail. All Israel from Dan even to Beersheba knew that

Samuel was confirmed as a prophet of the Lord (1 Samuel 3:19).

Like opening the curtains on a sunny morning, opportunities to minister are all around us, all the time. The Holy Spirit is always working and moving, and He wants to help us minister to others. This is why Jesus baptized us in the Holy Spirit's power. Hopefully, the six principles we just discussed will help you follow the Dove's leading and be willing to step out with more confidence in the days ahead. Just like a young waitress from Arizona.

Brooke was in her late twenties, and she had recently become a Christian. While attending our conference at her church in Arizona, she, along with about forty others, had received Spirit baptism during the Sunday night session. After the seekers had experienced the power of God and each one had enjoyed praying in the language of the Spirit for the first time, I gathered them together and encouraged them to use their new gift of supernatural ministry power. I said, "Pay attention to the people around you, and if anyone complains, simply offer to pray for the need. Try your best to do this in the next day or two, so you will see how easily this new power flows. God will prompt you to know what to say and do if you take the first step."

Pay attention to the people around you, and if anyone complains, simply offer to pray for the need.

The next night I asked for a few testimonies from people who had either been healed or baptized in the Holy Spirit the previous night. After a few healing testimonies, Brooke waved her hand. She explained, "Last night I was baptized in the Holy Spirit, and you [pointing to me] told us that we had a day or two to try out using the power, so I did it today. I'm a waitress, and as I was passing by one of my coworkers, I could see she was in pain. I asked her, 'Are you alright?' She went on to tell me how her back was in terrible pain, so I offered to pray for her. She agreed, so I put my hand on her shoulder and began to pray, not really knowing what to say. Almost immediately, my friend said, 'What is happening? My back is getting very warm all of the sudden.' I have never done this before, so I asked her if she wanted me to stop praying, but she replied, 'Finish up; the heat feels really good.' So, I finished my prayer."

Brooke continued, "The moment I stopped, she burst into tears and then began to straighten her back and legs against a nearby wall. She exclaimed, 'That is amazing! All my pain is gone, and my shoulders, hips and legs are flat against the wall. I have never been able to do that. I have severe scoliosis and have never been able to press my shoulders and hips flat against a wall at the same time before! How did you do that?' So, I told her about Jesus, and she prayed with me to get saved!"

The room erupted in applause, but Brooke interrupted the clapping with, "Wait a minute; I'm not done! When my shift was over, I was walking to the break room to clock out, and my manager passed me in the hall saying, 'Excuse me, but I'm getting a migraine, and I need to take my medicine immediately.' I walked quickly behind him and asked if I could pray, and he responded, 'I don't care what you do as long as you don't stop me from getting my medicine.' I walked right behind him, putting my hand on his shoulder, and started to pray for him. Almost immediately, he stopped and said, 'What are you doing? My head is suddenly getting very warm.' I told him, 'That's okay. It's supposed to do that,' and I finished my prayer. He was standing in a state of shock when he said, 'The migraine is gone! How did you do that?' So, I told him about Jesus, and he got saved too."

The auditorium went wild with applause and people praising God! Brooke was not only baptized in the Holy Spirit; she was fluently operating in the power almost immediately, the way it is supposed to be. She had stepped out to help her friends, and the Holy Spirit stepped up to help her. She had not only prayed in tongues the night before, but now, the same Holy Spirit guided her English words to minister and lead two friends to Christ— who also healed them!

The Holy Spirit is always moving. Open the curtain of fear, allow the light of His mission to guide you and you will see His power moving all around you! Follow the Dove's gentle leading.

———————————————

"If the Holy Spirit can take over the subconscious with our consent and cooperation, then we have almighty power working at the basis of our lives. Then we can do anything we ought to do, go anywhere we ought to go, and be anything we ought to be."

E. Stanley Jones

"Men ought to seek with their whole hearts to be filled with the Spirit of God. Without being filled with the Spirit, it is utterly impossible that an individual Christian or church can ever live or work as God desires."

Andrew Murray

Reflection questions:

1. How much activity of the Holy Spirit is available at any given time around us?

2. Interact with the six principles outlined in this chapter. How have you already discovered them to be true?

3. If you are in a room with others right now, look around the room and quietly ask the Holy Spirit if He wants to talk to someone there. Ask for His leading and help.

Chapter Nine

The Chicken-Dove Gauge

Several years ago, I was speaking at a church service and, afterwards, was casually talking with people in the foyer. There were only a few people remaining when a lady approached to shake my hand. She had a large white bandage taped over her nose, and her eyes were black and blue. I immediately wondered what had happened to cause such an injury. My mind began to turn, thinking of some of the possibilities. As she was getting ready to walk away, I ventured to ask her, "What happened to your nose?" She immediately looked down, apparently embarrassed about either the injury or how she had been injured.

She said, "I'd rather not say."

I certainly wanted to respect her privacy, but her guarded response made me very uneasy about her personal safety. This led me to suspect possible abuse, so I carefully asked her, "I do not want to pry, but are you safe?"

She immediately smiled and laughingly said, "Oh yes; I'm fine. No one hit me; this is just a crazy accident." After a brief pause, she said, "I haven't told anyone this because it is rather embarrassing, but I will tell you." Then she began to unfold a bizarre tale.

She said, "I live alone in an apartment and am a bit of a neat freak. I was cleaning my refrigerator a few days ago. It is the style of fridge where the freezer is on top. As I had the bottom door open, I decided to scrub the rubber seal along the door hinge, so I walked around to the side of the fridge and began to scrub it from the outside. There was one spot on the seal that would not scrub clean, so I leaned in to smell it to figure out what kind of stain it was. When I leaned in, I must have bumped the door. Right as my nose was pressed against the seal, the door slammed shut, pinching my nose between the seal and the closed door. I was totally trapped! I reached around the front of the door to grab the handle, but my nose was stuck on the opposite side, and I couldn't quite grasp the handle or get enough leverage to open the door myself. I started to yell, "HELP!" but no one on my floor was home. Finally, after about an hour of yelling, someone came to my rescue and opened the door. Nothing was broken, but my nose was swollen and bruised."

She was laughing—and so was I, not at her misfortune, but at the unfortunate chain of circumstances. Murphy's Law, which succinctly says, "Anything that can go wrong will go wrong," had struck again!

Speaking of things going wrong, have you ever run out of gas in your vehicle? Perhaps you looked at the fuel gauge and thought to yourself, "It will be close, but I should be able to arrive at my destination. I can make it."

Famous last words. That moment of overconfidence may have once cost me a six-mile walk in the rain to the nearest gas station…and back.

I have a feeling that there are a lot of you who have taken similar steps to try to make the remaining fuel last as long as possible. Perhaps you slowed down and turned off the air conditioner, hoping to save gas and thereby reduce as much risk of failure as possible. Lesson learned; do not take the risk when you think the tank is not sufficiently full. Do not tempt Murphy's Law.

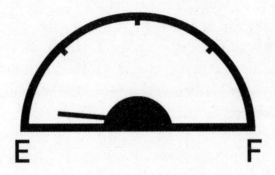

Risk could lead to embarrassing outcomes, like your nose being trapped in the fridge!

Fear of an Empty Tank

However, risk is a part of life. Success in life will require risk. As the saying goes, "No risk, no reward." The fear of risk has paralyzed countless people's natural potential and spiritual potential. Because we are so afraid of running out of gas (when we try to push the envelope), or the misfortune of a bruised nose (when we are not aware of the potential problems ready to snare us), we most often try to avoid any type of risk. Once again, the chicken rules.

But do not forget the Dove! His empowering gives us the ability to override the cowering paralysis of the inner chicken. Do you remember the five big reasons why we excuse ourselves from outward ministry? Here they are again:

1. I do not know what to do.
2. I do not have the training/education.

3. I do not have the resources.
4. I do not have the time.
5. I will make mistakes.

The Holy Spirit's supernatural ability gives us the universal antidote to any fear or limitation we may possess. He knows what to do. He has all knowledge and skill. He has all resources. He created time and has perfect timing. He does not make mistakes, but even if we make them, He gives us the wisdom to navigate through the effects caused by those mistakes.

Because our humanity is plagued by fear, many find it difficult to adjust to the "new normal" of Holy Spirit possibilities after they have experienced Spirit baptism. Because of fear, we do not try to step into new ways of conducting our lives, and we are hesitant to follow those new promptings of the Spirit. Though the Spirit baptism was a legitimate, significant moment, we wonder: How much help can we expect in the days ahead?

The Chicken-Dove Gauge

Just like a nearly-empty fuel gauge can cause us to enter "risk management" mode, the thought that we do not have enough spiritual power can cause us to slow down and reject any possible risk. Why would we even try to step out if the possibility of failure was greater than the possibility of success?

Please allow me to modify the fuel gauge and use it as a metaphor for measuring spiritual bravery. On the empty side, the fear side, is the chicken. On the full, confident side is the Dove.

According to the words of Jesus in Acts 1:8, when we are Spirit baptized, we receive power—our "Confidence Tank" is full although our emotional/logical perception of this fullness may be inaccurate.

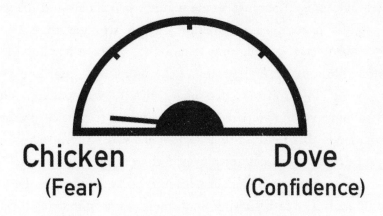

Above: What our emotions and logical perceptions may feel.

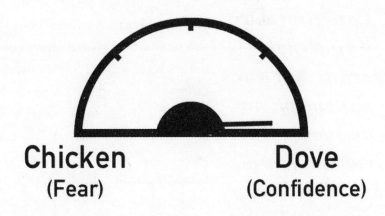

Above: What the true, spiritual reality is after Spirit baptism.

In spiritual reality, we receive more anointing or empowering than ever before at Spirit baptism, but often our gauges do not give us an accurate reading because of our own misunderstandings and misgivings. If we start our walk in the Spirit with a false concept, it will continue to affect our future perceptions. For example, when I was praying to be baptized in the Spirit, I was often discouraged because so many other seekers around me were apparently experiencing something much stronger than I was. They were crying, laughing, trembling or experiencing other noticeable, outward phenomena. I was quietly, gently experiencing the Holy Spirit in a personally powerful way, but apparently not as much when compared to the boisterous responses of others. I concluded that because their experience was more noticeable, it must be more significant or powerful than mine. Not true.

Just like the Spirit's supernatural empowering in the Old Testament, I was assuming that there were still categories of people who could receive dramatically and different spiritual possibilities. Do you remember my childhood experience of expecting a juicy steak dinner but getting a burnt hot dog? The old way was just for special leaders only, but with the salvation Jesus brought came the open door for every believer to experience the same access to the Spirit's power. As Acts 2:4 says, "And everyone present was filled with the Holy Spirit and began speaking in other languages as the Holy Spirit gave them this ability."

Correcting our internal narrative of fear, misconceptions and doubt will enable us to walk by the Spirit, not by our feelings.

I had assumed that not only did some Spirit baptisms come with higher voltage (because of more caffeinated outward response), but that these baptisms were infused with a higher level of ministry boldness or confidence. Biblically, that is not true. There is no emotional response accompanying the Baptism mentioned in the Bible. It certainly could happen, but it is peripheral to the whole experience. It is the same Jesus pouring out the same Holy Spirit on us; though we may respond differently, we are receiving the identical biblical gift with the identical biblical potential. Correcting our internal narrative of fear, misconceptions and doubt will enable us to walk by the Spirit, not by our feelings.

We must learn to calibrate our bravery gauge according to the always-reliable Scriptures instead of our often-unreliable feelings or conjecture. More feelings do not necessarily mean more power, nor does the absence of feelings mean the absence of power.

How the Tank Fills

The Spirit's power is like the gas in the tank. It is the power to help us serve God and others. Receiving the Spirit is often referred to as "being filled," "baptism" or "filling."

An important issue to consider is about the timing of receiving Spirit baptism. Is it an event or a process? Or both? It is an event in the sense that something happens at a certain time and place, but we must step back and see the process involved.

Acts 2 records the original participants and their activity on the Day of Pentecost outpouring. These participants were from Galilee (2:7). They had not been home to check on their families, businesses or responsibilities for at least a week, possibly much longer. At the ascension of Jesus, He told them to stay in the city of Jerusalem until they received the Spirit's power:

> "And now I will send the Holy Spirit, just as
> my Father promised. But stay here in the city
> until the Holy Spirit comes and fills you with
> power from heaven." Then Jesus led them to
> Bethany, and lifting his hands to heaven, He
> blessed them. While He was blessing them,

He left them and was taken up to heaven. So they worshiped Him and then returned to Jerusalem filled with great joy. And they spent all of their time in the Temple, praising God (Luke 24:49-53).

The Holy Spirit would not be poured out for another week; they could have gone home to Galilee, about 60 miles to the north. They could have checked their mail, mowed the grass and been back in Jerusalem in time for the Pentecost feast. Instead, they left the Ascension and went right back to Jerusalem to obey the command of Jesus to stay in Jerusalem until they were filled with the Holy Spirit. The moment their sandals turned away from Galilee and aimed toward Jerusalem, they made a decision to step into the process of being filled with the Holy Spirit's power. It is the same with us today.

From the instant we realize our need for supernatural ability to minister to others, and then start crying out to God for supernatural empowerment for that ministry, we step into the process of being filled with the Holy Spirit. Filling the tank begins. Somewhere along the line, sooner or later, we experience the confirming sign of tongues, which gives us confidence to try speaking to others on behalf of God. In that moment we can say we have been baptized in the Holy Spirit and our tank is technically full. However, the moment we first speak in tongues, we should not stop seeking to be filled with the Spirit. If anything, it should stir a greater hunger for more of the Holy Spirit in our lives. Ephesians 5:18 encourages us to "Be filled with the Spirit." The original Greek for "be filled" essentially means "remain in the state of being filled" or "be continuously filled." Paul is instructing us to continue in a lifelong pursuit of the Spirit's filling. Pursuing the fullness of the Spirit never ends. Besides that, we need to not just be full, but we need to overflow!

When we begin to seek, we begin to receive. It should not be viewed as a one-time event where we have nothing and then suddenly get something, but rather a lifetime pursuit with constant increase of the Spirit in our lives. If you have been seeking to be filled with the Holy Spirit, your gauge is reading more fully every time you seek. However, once it reads "full," you must keep on receiving to remain full. Constantly being filled is the goal.

Constantly being filled is the goal.

Remarkable Confirmation

I grew up in a traditional Pentecostal church in Harrisburg, Pennsylvania. Our church was very balanced and we were blessed with rock solid leadership. The Holy Spirit was free to move, but our pastors were careful to keep things in biblical order. Sunday night was always the best service of the week, with extended worship, challenging messages and powerful prayer times afterward. My family would enter into the prayer times, leaving our seats and moving, along with most of the crowd, to the altar area near the platform. During those prayer times, many wonderful things happened. People would give their lives to Jesus and experience healings and miracles. Some would pray in a kneeling position; others would stand or pace as they prayed. Some would pray very quietly; others would raise their voice. One gentleman would often pace the altar area and pray in a volume that others could hear, but not so loud that he distracted others. This man was not the most highly educated person in our church, but he really walked with God. Often, he and many others would appropriately pray in tongues during these times.

Please allow me to give a bit of a qualifier at this point. I would typically never repeat what someone else prayed in tongues, simply because it is sacred. I would not want to ever grieve the Holy Spirit by abusing something sacred that He gave to someone else. Understanding my reverence for the precious Holy Spirit and His gifts, I am going to tell you what this very spiritual man said when he would pray in tongues. Week after week, he would pace the altar calling on God with tears streaming down his face. He would pray these words. "Sheekimo Baba, Sheekimo Baba." I must confess that as a child the repetition of these words, over and over, week after week really stuck in my mind. Over the years, I have often remembered this godly gentleman's passionate prayers. It was easy to remember because this scenario (with these same details) occurred consistently over a period of years throughout my childhood.

Several years ago, we began to minister in very remote areas of Africa. During that time we developed a very close-knit relationship with a missionary couple in Tanzania, Gil and Dolfi Maunda. The Maundas are incredibly effective in ministering to tribal groups that have previously been very resistant to the Gospel. About a year ago, we were ministering in Tanzania alongside the Maundas, and one night we were having a prayer meeting on the outskirts of the Serengeti. This was a very passionate time of prayer with other pastors. We were worshipping and praying, both in our native languages as well as praying in tongues. Gil Maunda was standing near me, and suddenly I heard him begin to pray, "Sheekimo Baba, Sheekimo Baba!"

My vivid childhood memories of hearing those same words nearly overwhelmed me. Because of my feelings of sacred reverence for the language of the Spirit, I was reticent to say anything to Gil, but my curiosity hit an apex, and I had to ask him, "Gil, were you praying in tongues tonight?"

Gil responded, "I was praying back and forth in Swahili and tongues. Why do you ask, Tim?"

I responded, "A few moments ago, you were praying …saying some words I don't understand, but words that I have heard before—"Sheekimo Baba.""

"Yes, Tim," Gil said, "that part was in Swahili, not tongues."

Stunned, I said, "Swahili? Those words are not tongues?"

"No," Gil said, "let me translate them into English for you. 'Sheekimo' means 'to give someone the highest honor,' like to an elder or respected guest. 'Baba' is the word for 'Daddy' or 'Papa.' I was just telling my Father in heaven that I was honoring Him." The literal translation of "sheekimo" is "I grasp your feet."[12]

I could hardly believe my ears! In my home church, that godly but uneducated man had been yielding to the Holy Spirit's language. He did not have a clue what he was saying, but he was making a profound statement of worship and adoration to his Heavenly Father. Tears of gratitude filled my eyes as I pondered the wonder-filled ways of God.

I have often listened to myself as I pray in tongues. To be honest, it sounds like nonsense to my intellect. From my youngest age, I have learned English one word at a time, associating each with a known concept. Each word of a foreign language represents intellectually intentional nouns, verbs and other parts of speech. However, when I speak in tongues, my intellect is not satisfied

---

[12] The actual Kiswahili spelling is "shikamo," but is pronounced "shee-kim-o" for American English speakers.

because I have not learned the meaning to the words I am speaking. Paul said,

> For if I pray in tongues, my spirit is praying, but I don't understand what I am saying. Well then, what shall I do? I will pray in the spirit, and I will also pray in words I understand (1 Corinthians 14:14-15).

In other words, the general rule of praying in the Spirit is that it is not intellectually satisfying, but rather, it is spiritually satisfying. Paul's conclusion is that just because he did not understand what was being said (in tongues) did not mean that he would refuse to participate. Paul "willed" to speak in both the known and unknown language because each satisfy a different part of our being. For someone to say, "I will never pray in tongues because it is nonsense," is a confession that they trust their knowledge over Scriptures. We must learn to humbly submit our intellect to the Holy Spirit.

Praying in the Spirit is not intellectually satisfying, but rather, it is spiritually satisfying.

When praying in the Spirit, I am trusting the prompting of the Holy Spirit to enable me to pray, trusting Him to the point of intellectual abandonment. There are isolated times when someone may experience a situation where the language is understood, but usually, we must be willing to yield our voice to the inner nudge and step out in faith, without any intellectual verification afterwards.

178

Do you see how praying in the Spirit constantly trains our mind, will and emotions to submit to the Holy Spirit? The more I pray in the Spirit, the more I submit my thoughts and will to God, for I am saying the words He is leading me to say, not the ones I want to speak. But how can this practice translate into real-life ministry? Let me introduce you to Karl.

Karl

Karl was a young father when he was forced to kiss his young bride goodbye. He had been drafted into the Second World War and had to report for duty, leaving his wife and daughter alone. The war was traumatic for everyone involved, including Karl. He began his service by landing on the fourth wave at D-Day. His final assignment was guarding Hitler's vacant "Eagles Nest" headquarters. He was involved in freeing a prison camp and witnessed the atrocities of the Nazis firsthand. When he returned home, he was deeply distressed. Today, he would likely be diagnosed with Post Traumatic Stress Disorder, but in the 1940s, he was simply told he had "war fatigue" and was sent home with a disability compensation. Once reunited with his family after several years of absence, the terrible memories continued to haunt Karl. Trying to dull the pain, he began to drink heavily, and when drunk, Karl would become violent to his daughter and especially abusive toward his wife. When sobered up, he was often remorseful, yet he continued the alcohol/abuse cycle for years. His wife began to break. The constant fear and anxiety, along with the cumulative effects of physical abuse, had finally reached a critical stage. Suffering a nervous breakdown, she was hospitalized, and she would be in and out of institutions until her premature death. The daughter, and later a new son, would bounce from the care of their father to other relatives and back again. The drinking and abuse continued.

When his daughter, Ruth, was about twelve years old, Karl became violently drunk and threatened to kill her. She remembers running down their apartment stairs saying, "I'll never come back! I'll never come back!" Ruth had given her life to Jesus sometime earlier, because a school friend had reached out to her. She began to attend a nearby church and had connected with her Sunday School teachers, who were not able to have kids of their own. After several years, they took Ruth into their home and loved her as their own daughter. Ruth lost contact with her father and brother, but she would have the unspeakable joy of leading her mother to Jesus before her untimely passing.

Karl became violently drunk and threatened to kill her.

I know this story well because Ruth is my mother and Karl was my grandfather. My memories of him began when I was about ten years old, when a stranger rang our doorbell and I answered. A man I had never seen before greeted me through the screen door and asked if there was a "Ruthie who lived at this house." I asked him to wait while I went to look for my mom. When she saw her dad standing on the porch, it had been about twenty-five years since she had run for her life from his drunken rage. They talked cordially for some time, avoiding the obvious. Then, just as unexpectedly as he had arrived, he abruptly left.

My mother was raised outside of New York City, but when she and my father married, they set up house in central Pennsylvania. My grandfather Karl had found his daughter in another state with a different last name and was hoping to reconnect on some level. With that awkward visit under our belt, my parents gathered my sisters and I and had a family meeting. During that meeting, my mother told us much more of the story about her birth dad. (I say birth dad because the couple who taught my mother's Sunday School class and later took her in, the Williamsons, were the only grandparents I had ever known. They were wonderful Christians and filled with joy and kindness. It seemed that God replaced the sorrow of my mother's early years by giving her ideal adoptive parents who loved, listened to and cared for her.) In that family meeting, my mother asked us to pray for her father's salvation, which was a commitment we took seriously.

Over the next ten years, my grandfather would show up on the doorstep—unannounced, just like he had done before. With every surprise visit, my family's resolve to lead him to the Lord grew, and so did our efforts. Even though I was only a child, I wrote him a letter that explained how he could give his life to Jesus, but there was no response from him. I sent him several Bibles in the mail, again, no response. I studied two famous evangelism courses with the intent of leading him to Jesus, but the attempts to follow the plan failed. One time, he hung up the phone on me and another time at our house, while I was sharing with him, he simply got up from his chair and left the room. I had tried everything I knew to do.

Several years later, after Rochelle and I had married, I received a phone call from my mother. She had been talking to her dad, and he had informed her of his critical medical state. He had internal hemorrhaging, and he was receiving regular transfusions to replenish the blood loss, but the condition persisted. He was bracing for the inevitable. Rochelle and I happened to be speaking at a church conference in the Midwest when my mother called us about her dad's condition. After I hung up the phone, I began to pray, "Lord, send someone to him, there in the outskirts of New York City, to minister to him." Honestly, I felt that my responsibility to lead him to Christ was lifted because of his repeated rejections of my attempts to lead him to Jesus. When I prayed that "Here I am, Lord, but send someone else" kind of prayer, the Holy Spirit deeply convicted me about my lack of responsibility for my lost grandfather. I began to pray again, replaying all my failed attempts of face-to-face conversations, phone calls, sending Bibles and letters, all ending in rejection. In desperation, I prayed, "God, I have tried unsuccessfully many times; I have told him everything I know to say." Immediately the Holy Spirit whispered back into my spirit, "That is the problem; you have been speaking only what you have wanted to say. Will you allow me to speak to him?"

I was overwhelmed with feelings of inadequacy and fear. Even though I knew the confidence gauge was full, my emotions and intellect were saying it was empty. Who would I listen to? After spending some time in prayer, I knew what had to be done. I was speaking at a conference in the Midwest, but I had to change our plans and get to the New York City area as soon as possible. And, within a day or so, we were on our way to see my Grandfather Karl, praying that he would be well enough to see us—and willing to do so. There were no guarantees.

Driving about fifteen hundred miles in two days was not easy nor pleasant, and I found myself at a total loss for words of prayer. Since I had already told my grandfather nearly everything I could think of saying about Jesus, I found myself praying in the Spirit for most of the drive. The more I prayed, the more confidence filled my life. I was not sure exactly what was going to happen, but my confidence tank was full, and I was ready to find out.

When we pulled into a suburban New York mall parking lot, I said one final prayer and then sent Rochelle and our boys inside. They called our friends and family to pray. My grandfather pulled his purple Plymouth into the mall's parking lot, right beside our vehicle. He was so weak I had to help him put the car into park. His face was skeletal, and he was obviously very, very ill. I helped him into our vehicle and sat down beside him. I still had no clue what to say or where to start, but I had been praying in the Spirit for extended periods of time the last few days, so I was well-practiced in yielding to the Holy Spirit. I was filled with a wonderful mixture of self-fear and God-confidence, as I have found it to typically be.

We exchanged cordial greetings, then I said, "Grandfather, I need to say something to you." The statement was true; I did need to say something. The problem was that my emotional/intellectual reading on my confidence gauge was perhaps at an all-time low. I felt nothing. No electricity; no power. Even though it felt like the gauge was all the way on the chicken/fear side, I took a deep breath and surrendered my speech to Jesus—just the way I would pray in tongues, but this time in English. I do not remember the exact words, but they were not very impressive to me. In fact, some of the things I wrote to him in a previous letter felt much more convincing than what I had just said. My mind began to race about how I could rescue this incredibly important moment of eternal destiny.

These thoughts were interrupted by my grandfather brokenly asking, "How could Jesus ever forgive my sins after all the pain I have caused my family?" Then his bottom lip began to quiver as the tears began to streak down his face.

I was stunned. Everything I needed to say to him then just seemed to flow from my heart with ease. Within a matter of

183

minutes, he was praying with me to accept Christ with tear-filled eyes. After we had prayed, I told him how Jesus could also heal his body, to which his surprised reply was, "No fooling?" I prayed with him for healing, and although I did not sense overwhelming power, he felt something. He told me of how his pain was subsiding. We silently hugged for a long time. Nothing needed to be said. It was an overwhelmingly emotional moment. One of the greatest joys of my life was to call my mom and tell her that her father had surrendered his life to Christ!

About a week later, my parents took a trip to visit my grandfather. He was no longer pale and skeletal. The change in his personality was dramatic. He had gone to his doctor and was told that his incurable condition had been cured. The hemorrhaging had miraculously stopped. Jesus had healed him—no fooling.

Within a short while, he moved close to my parents' house, and my mother and father cared for him. This was one of the most redemptive, healing parts of the miracle. Grandfather would go to church and pray, and you would even catch him saying, "Praise the Lord," when something went well. He lived for about six years before he went to be with the Lord. I am crying as I type these words: He went to be with the Lord.

My grandfather's story is not the exception to the rule. Jesus has paid the price for your family and friends—and strangers—to enter heaven. He is willing that none should perish (1 Peter 3:20). The reason why we need the power of the Holy Spirit is simply to overcome our innate chicken fear, selfishness, excuses, inabilities and inadequacies. This is why the Dove empowers our lives with confidence and ministry ability. We do not have to know what to do; that is His job. Even when we feel like our gauge is empty, He is always present to assist us in making Jesus real to others.

So now it is up to you.

Have you been baptized in the Holy Spirit yet? If not, turn to the appendix and read, "How to Receive Spirit Baptism." Jesus will fill you. Today.

If you have already been baptized in the Holy Spirit, why not do something with it? Today, spend a few moments worshipping Jesus, then, as you are able, allow your will to yield to the supernatural language of tongues. Relax. Let it flow boldly, loudly. Absorb the process while you are choosing to yield your act of speaking to the Holy Spirit's prompting. This is how He may likely lead you to speak to others. Praying in tongues is the way to accurately test the gauge for your confidence tank, not going by what you may or may not feel.

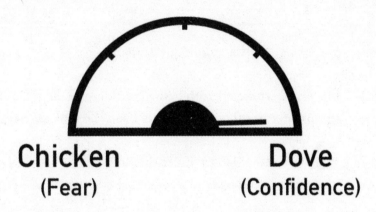

Chicken   Dove
(Fear)   (Confidence)

When you speak those heavenly (yet foolish-sounding) words, you are proving that the supernatural power of the Spirit is upon your life. Trust Him. Trust His power. Release the chicken of fear and embrace the Dove of the Holy Spirit. He wants to help you with His supernatural ability. Step out from behind the curtain of pride, and allow God to amaze you.

"Being filled with the Holy Spirit is simply this—having my whole nature yielded to His power. When the whole soul is yielded to the Holy Spirit, God Himself will fill it."

Andrew Murray

"When you strip it of everything else, Pentecost stands for power and life. That's what came into the church when the Holy Spirit came down on the day of Pentecost."

David Wilkerson

Reflection questions:

1. Have you struggled with being confident in stepping out to minister to others? What has been the typical result?

2. Have you struggled to discern the difference between Holy Spirit courage and intellectual concern/fear?

3. What resolution can you honestly make concerning the next opportunity to step out and minister to someone else?

Appendix

How to Receive Spirit Baptism

Receiving the baptism in the Holy Spirit is actually very easy. Jesus desires to baptize and we desire everything He has for us. We are desiring His will for us.

The only qualification needed to experience Spirit baptism is that you are saved. Aside from that, there is nothing else that you need before you begin to ask Jesus to fill you with His Spirit. If you are struggling with some sort of sin issue, ask Jesus for fresh forgiveness and proceed to seek Him, He will not withhold His Spirit's power from you. You and I need His power so urgently in our lives.

The most important step in receiving the Baptism is to get as close to Jesus, the Baptizer, as you can.

Do you feel more freedom when you pray in the company of others? Then call a few friends to pray with you. Do you find that praying alone enables you to have fewer distractions and less self-consciousness? Then get alone to pray. Either way, Jesus will meet with you.

Here are the three phases in receiving Spirit baptism:

1. Vulnerability;
2. Awareness;
3. Cooperation.

1. Vulnerability

There is an underlying principle in receiving anything from God: vulnerability. Vulnerability toward God involves us humbling ourselves when receiving from Him. How did you and I experience salvation? We first realized that we could not fix our own sin problem and then called on Jesus to save us. We humbled ourselves and prayed. If you have received a physical or emotional healing in the past, what did you do to welcome this miracle? Very likely you prayed. The Bible says that "Anyone who wants to come to Him must believe that God exists and that He rewards those who sincerely seek Him" (Hebrews 11:6). We receive from God most often through prayer. If you want to be baptized in the Holy Spirit, you will need to draw near in prayer. Prayer is a state of vulnerability. Prayer says, "I cannot meet this need in my life, but I believe God can." As the Scripture above explains, the reason we come to God is because we believe that He exists and responds to our seeking.

Our job in receiving anything from God is to become increasingly more vulnerable with Him. Pray out loud, lift your hands, voice your passion for Him and do not hold yourself back. Give your best effort to lowering your guard, moment by moment trying to yield more and more to Him. Raise your voice a decibel or two and lift your hands an inch higher. You may need to pray vulnerable prayers, expressing how much you need God. Do it for a few minutes before you sense the next phase beginning to happen.

2. Awareness

After some time of vulnerable, vocal prayer, you will begin to become aware of the Holy Spirit's presence falling upon you or stirring you deeply. Jesus is responding as you cry out vulnerably.

His presence will not scare you. You will not be out of control. You will recognize His presence because you have sensed Him before, but most likely your new awareness of His presence will be somewhat stronger than usual.

You may sense that He falls upon you, then His presence lifts. This is not because you have made a mistake; this is a common experience. You will find that if you choose to draw near in vulnerability again, His presence will fall upon you again.

He is surrounding you with His presence so you will have just enough courage to know that He is with you as you step into the final phase.

3. Cooperation

Now that the Holy Spirit is being poured out upon you, you must learn to cooperate with His gentle leading. He will not make you speak in tongues; you must learn to follow His promptings. He will nudge you and give you just enough faith to try to speak out in the new language, but you must choose to cooperate with Him and try to do so. Your goal is to offer your physical ability to speak for His use, not yours. As long as you are speaking words and sentences you understand in English (or whatever languages you may know), you will be speaking out of your brain and intelligence. Your goal is to try to speak out of your Spirit where He is stirring you.

Often, at this point, people begin to experience different types of prompting from the Holy Spirit. Typically, they will get a prompting of some strange sounds or syllables. This is when they should begin to speak. If this happens, say them out loud. Your intelligence will try to talk you out of it, but trust the Holy Spirit's leading when He is upon you! Sometimes people feel a physical urge to speak but are not quite sure what to say. Cooperate with this physical prompting; take a step of faith, and try to give your raw sound to this inner prompting. You may grunt or sputter for a few moments, but relax and you will find new syllables beginning to emerge. Yield to the new words; let them flow.

Trust the Holy Spirit's leading when He is upon you!

You will find that when you begin to speak in this new, unknown language, your mind can still think and may even begin to try to rationalize what is happening. This is normal. Paul explained,

"For if I pray in a tongue, my spirit is praying,
but I don't understand what I am saying"
(1 Corinthians 14:14).

You will not understand the words you are speaking. It is normal to have a mix of intellectual questions and spiritual sensation. Your brain will not like the new language and will likely doubt its authenticity; your spirit will be released in a new way, and you will likely sense an inner strength.

From this day forward, you can start and stop speaking in tongues as easily as choosing to yield to the Spirit or not. You do not need to yell or cry; sometimes our emotions connect, and sometimes they do not. Emotions (or the lack of them) do not validate the concrete sign that He has given to you.

Whenever you are praying in the Spirit, you are practicing yielding your voice to the Holy Spirit's prompting. It will become more and more natural for you to follow Him in the days ahead.

If You Feel Like You Are Struggling...

Sometimes it can feel difficult to receive something from God because of our misunderstandings or sense of overwhelming unworthiness. I witnessed one of the most remarkable Spirit baptisms of my life in the city of Rome, Italy. It was New Year's Day, and I was speaking at a church which met on the ground floor of a high-rise apartment building. Many of those in attendance were brand new Christians. After teaching about the Holy Spirit, I invited those who wanted to be filled with His power to step forward to the front of the church. Among them was a lady in her early forties who, by outward appearance, did not live a life of luxury and privilege. While I was praying for each person to be filled, I noticed her standing motionless, with eyes closed and hands clasped in silent prayer. After several minutes, I heard her begin to melodically speak in a supernatural language, but the way she was doing it was most unusual. She would stretch one hand toward the ceiling and then draw that hand to her heart, and then she would do the same with her other hand. She was alternating this hand motion, one after another, and each time she would speak a word in tongues.

After the prayer time was over, the pastor called for testimonies of those who had been healed or filled with the Holy Spirit during the prayer time. After a few healing testimonies, this lady stepped forward to share her experience, "I was raised as an orphan and have lived a very hard life. I don't recall ever hearing someone tell me that they loved me, and I have never received a gift. As I was standing here tonight praying, I was telling Jesus, 'I don't know how to receive gifts, let alone the gift of the Holy Spirit. Please help me.' After a few minutes of praying this, I had an incredible thing happen.   Jesus was suddenly standing in front of me! I could see Him, and He was holding a large bundle of beautiful flowers. He handed me a single flower, and because no one has ever given me flowers before, I experienced His love in a new, profound way. I felt a surge of love in my heart like I have not before known. As I reached up to grab the flower, that surge of love in my heart became a word on my lips. I wanted to say 'I love you' to Jesus, but each time He handed me a beautiful flower, a new word in tongues came from my lips. He kept on handing me flowers, and each time I went to say 'I love you' a new word in tongues would come out instead."

Jesus is the one who baptizes us in the Holy Spirit. If you feel like you are struggling or that there are a million reasons why you can't experience this gift, it's alright. Jesus wants to empower you with His Spirit. He will help you, and He will fill you. He will navigate around any barriers you put up and any hang-ups you have, as long as you continue to pray and receive the gift you don't feel you deserve. And don't ever stop seeking to be filled. Ever.